YEOMANRY REGULATIONS;

BEING AN ABRIDGMENT OF THE

REGULATIONS FOR THE FORMATIONS AND MOVEMENTS OF THE CAVALRY,

ADAPTED TO THE USE OF YEOMANRY CORPS;

WITH

SUGGESTIONS ON DISCIPLINE AND INTERIOR; AND RULES FOR PATROLS, PICQUETS, AND MEASURES OF PRECAUTION IN TIMES OF DISTURBANCE;

ALSO,

THE FORMS OF YEOMANRY RETURNS; AND AN ABSTRACT OF THE REGULATIONS ISSUED BY THE GOVERNMENT DEPARTMENTS CONNECTED WITH YEOMANRY.

A NEW EDITION, REVISED IN CONFORMITY WITH
THE CAVALRY REGULATIONS OF

1844.

The Naval & Military Press Ltd

Published by

The Naval & Military Press Ltd
Unit 10 Ridgewood Industrial Park,
Uckfield, East Sussex,
TN22 5QE England

Tel: +44 (0) 1825 749494
Fax: +44 (0) 1825 765701

www.naval-military-press.com
www.military-genealogy.com
www.militarymaproom.com

In reprinting in facsimile from the original, any imperfections are inevitably reproduced and the quality may fall short of modern type and cartographic standards.

PREFACE.

In offering the following pages to the Yeomanry, a body of men, to the patriotic and zealous services of whom the country has been so often indebted for the preservation of the rights and properties of the subject, it may be well to give some explanation of the views with which this Abridgment has been compiled, and the object it is intended to forward.

There cannot be a more various organization than that of the British Yeomanry Corps. Some Regiments which have been long established are on a footing of discipline hardly susceptible of improvement. Others of more recent formation are in circumstances of great difficulty as to interior arrangement, and the utmost exertion and activity on the part of their Officers will be necessary for years, before they can be brought to the perfection of the older corps. Several Regiments of Yeomanry can number as many as six, eight, and even ten Troops, a body so numerous as hardly to be within the management of a regimental staff of the usual establishment, and these too dispersed over a great extent of country, and seldom assembled regimentally for exercise. Their means of obtaining instruction are also very limited, and the Troop Serjeant-Majors, although generally an experienced, zealous, and intelligent class of men, yet from want of practice must necessarily lose some of their knowledge of field duty.

Besides the embodied Regiments, there are a great number of independent Troops of Yeomanry in various parts of the country, the individuals of which, from having fewer opportunities of comparison, and consequently less spirit of rivalry than exists among the embodied Regiments, are in many cases far less advanced in acquaintance with their field duty. The degree of proficiency is quite as various in the officers and men in general as in the different corps.

There are to be found in the ranks of the Yeomanry many Officers and Non-commissioned Officers, who, from former service in the regular Cavalry, are perfectly competent to all points of regimental duty and command. Another description of Officer in the Yeomanry consists of gentlemen, who, from a natural military taste, or from a laudable desire to perform well whatever they take in hand, and to qualify themselves for the command which their position in their own neighbourhood leads them to assume in these corps, have made themselves nearly or quite as much masters of their business as if they had gone through the whole gradation of instruction in the Regiments of the Line. But on the other hand there are many Yeomanry Officers who, from necessary avocations, and totally different pursuits, are unable to follow up their detail of duty, although anxious to promote the advantage of their corps, and proud to appear in the ranks of such respectable unions. And it must not be forgotten, that however efficient and active their Officers may be, the very short periods allotted for the training of Yeomanry will not admit of much of that practical instruction by which the Cavalry recruit is usually formed.

The existing Regulation of the Cavalry must always be the standard for the guidance of Yeomanry; but enough has been said to show, that however essential for reference and useful to the Officer who has made field movements his peculiar study, still as a manual for the Troop Serjeant-Major, by which to drill the detached Troop, or as a guide for the Officer who has recently enrolled himself in a Regiment of Yeomanry, and desires to arrive at the necessary degree of acquaintance with his duty to enable him to acquit himself creditably, the Cavalry Regulation may, by some abridgment in its details, be made more easy of acquirement without injury to its principles. Indeed, there is much of that Regulation which, however essential for regular Cavalry, may be considered quite inapplicable for Yeomanry, if only on the score of there not being time for acquiring it, however superficially. For instance, the period necessary in the Regulars to pass a recruit through the riding-school, and mount him in squadron, is from four to six months, and it very frequently happens that those country recruits who have been accustomed all their lives to horses, give the riding-master most trouble to initiate them in the details of Military Equitation.

The object, then, of this Abridgment is to make such a selection from the Cavalry Regulation as may enable Yeomanry corps of old standing, and whose members are for the most part conversant with the rudiments of Cavalry instruction, to follow up the system sufficiently to enable them to execute, when regimentally assembled, the most useful and ordinary movements, avoiding such parts of the Regulation as would seem unnecessary and ill-adapted for such Yeomanry corps, as are too much scattered to allow of their assembling often as entire Regiments for the purposes of field manœuvres.

At the end of the Abridgment are appended some suggestions for discipline and interior arrangement, with a short notice of the precautions most advisable for occasions of disturbance.

W. F. DE Ros, Lieut.-Col.
Major of Brigade to the Cavalry.

February 1, 1833.

CONTENTS.

PART THE FIRST.

	Page
SECT. I. Foot Drill	1
II. Inspection of a Troop on Foot	3
III. Practice of Field Movements on Foot	4
IV. Foot Parade of a Regiment	4
V. Duties of Sentries	6
VI. Directions for Funeral Parties	7
VII. Belts, Arms, Accoutrements, and Saddlery	9
VIII. Military Horsemanship	11
IX. Carbine Exercise on Foot	24
X. Carbine Exercise on Horseback	31
XI. Pistol Exercise on Horseback	35
XII. Sword Exercise	36
XIII. Officers' Salute, &c.	44

PART THE SECOND.

INSTRUCTION OF THE TROOP AND SQUADRON.

		Page
Sect. I.	Terms of Formation and Manœuvre	46
II.	Distances and Intervals	48
III.	Directions for Instructors	49
IV.	Dressing	50
V.	Marching to the Front	52
VI.	Inclining	54
VII.	Passaging and Reining Back	55
VIII.	Wheeling	55
IX.	Threes	58
X.	Paces	59
XI.	Formation of the Troop	60
XII.	Formation of the Squadron	62
XIII.	General Rules on the Marches and Formations by Threes and Files	69
XIV.	Marches to the Flanks, Front, and Rear, by Threes and Files	71
XV.	Formations to the Front, Flanks, and Rear, from Threes and Files	75
XVI.	Countermarch, and reversing the Front, of the Squadron	81
XVII.	Diminution and Increase of Front	82
XVIII.	Advance of the Squadron	89
XIX.	Preparation of the Squadron for Regimental Movement	91
XX.	Instruction of Officers	93
XXI.	Linking Horses	94
XXII.	Dismounted Service	95

PART THE THIRD.

FIELD MOVEMENTS, &c.

		Page
Sect. I.	Formation of the Regiment	107
II.	Post and Duties of Officers	107
III.	Commands	109
IV.	Principles of Field Movement	111
V.	Rules for Markers and Dressing	113
VI.	Taking up Points of Formation	117
VII.	March in Line, Direction, and Alignment	119
VIII.	Formation for Attack	121
IX.	The Charge or Attack	122
X.	Inspection or Review of the Regiment	124

Sect. XI.

MOVEMENTS FROM LINE.

No.		
1.	Change Front, Half Right	133
2.	Change Front to the Right	134
3.	Change Front, Half Right, Back	135
4.	Change Front, Right Back	136
5.	Change Front, Half Right, on the Second Squadron	137
6.	Change Front to the Right, on the Second Squadron	138
7.	By Threes, Change Position, Half Right	140
8.	By Threes, Change Position, Half Right Back	142
9.	Open Column of Troops to the Right	143
10.	Advance in Open Column from the Right	144
11.	Column of Troops from the Right in succession by the Rear	146

CONTENTS.

	Page
No. 12. Advance in Double Column from the Centre	147
13. Form Double Column on the Centre	148
14. Open Column in Rear of the Right	150
15. Close Column on the Second Squadron, Right in Front	152
17. Inverted Line to the Rear	154
18. Advance in Echellon from the Right	156
19. Retire by alternate Squadrons	158
20. Advance by Threes from the Right of Squadrons	160
21. Retire by Threes from the Right of Squadrons	161

Sect. XII.

MOVEMENTS FROM CLOSE COLUMN.

Observations on the Objects and Movements of the Close Column	163
No. 1. Deploy on the First Squadron	165
2. Deploy on the Third Squadron	166
3. Form Line to the Left on the Third Squadron	168
4. Change Front to the Right	169
5. The Column will Reverse its Front	170
6. The Squadrons will Countermarch	171

Sect. XIII.

MOVEMENTS FROM OPEN COLUMN.

Observations on the Objects and Movements of the Open Column	173
No. 1. Left Wheel into Line	175
2. Form Line to the Front	176
3. Form Line to the Front on the Rear Troop	177
4. Form Line to the Front on the Second Squadron	178
5. Form Line to the Rear on the Leading Troop	179
6. Form Line to the Rear on the Rear Troop	181

CONTENTS.

	Page
No. 7. Form Line to the Rear on the Second Squadron	182
8. Form Line to the Left on the New Alignment	183
9. Form Line to the Left on the New Alignment	184
10. To the Reverse Flank, Right form Line	185
11. Form Inverted Line to the Right, on the Heads of Squadrons	186
12. Form Inverted Line to the Front	187
13. Form Inverted Line to the Left on the First Squadron	189
14. Rear of the Column to the Front	190
15. Form Close Column	191
16. Form Line to the Front } from DOUBLE	192
17. Form Line to the Right } COLUMN	193

SECT. XIV. Skirmishing	194
XV. Advance Guards and Rear Guards	196
XVI. Arrangements on occasion of Riots or General Disturbances	197
XVII. Precautions on the March	200
XVIII. Escorts	203
XIX. Offences and Fines	209
XX. Abstract of the Government Regulations	213
XXI. Pay and Allowances applicable to Permanent Duty, or Duty in Aid of the Civil Power	223
XXII. Destruction or Loss of Arms	225
XXIII. Form of Return of Effective Strength	227

PART THE FIRST.

Section I. FOOT DRILL.

Position.

The body and shoulders should be square to the front; the heels together; the toes a little turned out; the arms hanging down easy by the sides; the breast advanced; the head upright; and the weight of the man bearing upon the ball of the foot.

On the word "*Stand at Ease,*" the right foot is drawn a few inches back; the left knee rather bent; and the hands joined in front, with the palm of the left over the back of the right hand.

On the word "*Attention,*" the proper position is resumed by letting the hands fall instantly by the sides, and bringing up the right foot.

On the word "*Eyes Right,*" or "*Eyes Left,*" a glance of the eyes only must be given to the hand ordered, without at all moving the head or shoulders.

The Facings.

In going through the facings, the left heel never quits the ground, the body must be a little inclined forward, and the knees straight.

"*Right Face.*" Place the hollow of the right foot against the left heel; then raise the toes, and turn to the right on both heels.

"*Left Face.*" Place the right heel against the hollow of the left foot; then raise the toes and turn to the left on both heels.

"*Right About, Face.*" Place the ball of the right foot against the left heel; then raise the toes, and turn to the right about on both heels, and replace the right foot in line with the left.

Yeomanry. B

"*Left About, Face.*" Place the right heel against the ball of the left foot; then raise the toes, and turn to the left about on both heels, and replace the right foot in line with the left.

Position in Marching.

"*Quick March.*" On the second word, step off with the left foot, with the body steady, the head upright, arms easy by the sides, and without any swinging; the leg stretched, but without stiffening the knee; the toe rather pointed, and the foot brought flat to the ground.

On the word "*Halt,*" finish the step, and remain steady.

On the word "*Right* (or *Left*) *Incline*" given while marching, make a half-turn to the hand ordered, and advance in that direction till the word "*Front, Turn;*" then resume the former direction.

Dressing should be taken up regularly, beginning from the flank ordered; each man should just see the surface of the face of the man next beyond him, the eyes only being turned, but the body square and upright.

Wheeling.

On the word "*Right* (or *Left*) *Wheel,*" the man on the standing flank faces in the direction ordered. On the word "*March,*" the remainder step off with their eyes turned to the wheeling flank, except the outward man of all, who looks towards the standing flank, lengthening his step a little; the others step shorter, in proportion as they are nearer to the man on the inward flank. After the wheel, "*Halt, Dress,*" is given.

For wheeling on the move, the word is given "*Right,*" or "*Left,*" followed by "*Forward,*" as soon as the wheel is completed.

Opening and Closing the Ranks.

The men being formed in two ranks at close order, that is, with one pace between the front and rear ranks, on the word

"*Rear Rank, take Order*," the right and left-hand men of the rear rank step back one pace, face to their right, and stand to mark the distance to which the rear rank is to step back; every other man remains ready to move. On the word "*March*," the flank men front, and the rear rank falls back one pace, dressing by the right the instant it is in its place. On the word "*Rear Rank—take Close Order—March*," the rank closes up again within one pace.

Section II.

INSPECTION OF A TROOP ON FOOT.

The men fall in according to size roll in two ranks, the tallest man on the right. The Troop is then numbered and divided into two Divisions. The ranks are opened by the usual word of command, and the Officer goes down each rank, the men showing their arms, whether carbine or pistol, and sending the ramrods into the barrels, to show if clean by the appearance of the end of the ramrod when withdrawn. The Officer should go through the ranks a second time, each man drawing and showing his sword, to see if they are firm in the hilt, and clean. At the same time he should observe the state of the belts and clothing, and require each man to show his ammunition properly secured.

After inspection, the ranks are closed, and the Troop is dismissed by the words,

"*Right Face—Lodge Arms.*" The whole face to the right, and drop their carbines to the port; the front rank break off to the left, the rear rank to the right, and quit the parade without noise.

N.B. In turning in a guard or picquet, the same mode is to be observed.

Section III.

PRACTICE OF FIELD MOVEMENTS ON FOOT.

For this purpose the Regiment is to be formed and told off in the same manner as when mounted, and the same system will be pursued throughout. The Officers are to be posted two paces in front of the Squadron, and the rear rank at the like distance from the front rank. In increasing the front, the "Double Time" will be used to represent the "Trot;" also in the wheels, when the pace of manœuvre is "Quick Time."

In the formations one pace is to be allowed for a horse's length.

Section IV.

FOOT PARADE OF A REGIMENT.

The Regiment is formed in Line in the same manner as when mounted, with intervals of one-fourth between Squadrons, and a distance of two paces between the front and rear rank. Squadron and Troop Leaders two paces before the front rank. Serrefiles the same distance behind the rear rank.

"*Rear Rank, take Order.*" The whole of the Officers recover their swords. On the word "*March*," the rear rank steps back one pace; the Squadron and Troop Leaders step one pace forward. The Squadron Serrefile comes to the front by an opening made for him by the right file of the left Troop. Troop Serrefiles move out round the flanks of Squadrons, and all place themselves as when mounted.

The whole of the Officers dress by the Troop Leaders of the "Squadron of Direction."

Having seen that the dressing is correct, the Adjutant gives a signal with his sword for all Officers to bring theirs to the "Port." (See p. 44.)

General Salute. "*Draw Swords.*" The men draw their

FOOT PARADE. 5

swords, and bring them down to the "Carry," Officers recovering and saluting with the two last motions.

After saluting, Officers bring their swords to the "Carry," taking the time from the Commanding Officer.

After inspection of the ranks, "*Rear Rank, take Close Order,*" the Officers recover swords, and face to the right.

"*March.*" Squadron and Troop Leaders take a side pace to the right, front, and slope swords.

"*March past in Slow Time,*" "*Threes Right,*" "*March.*" The Column marches past by Squadrons, each receiving the word "*Front, Forward,*" when it reaches the wheeling point, and Officers taking post as when mounted. The column being closed up after the third angle, passes in quick time, by marching off into Column of Troops the same as on horseback, and wheels into Line on reaching its original ground.

OBSERVATIONS. It may be well to remark, that to bestow too much time and attention upon the Foot Parade of a Regiment would by no means be judicious. The only reason in fact for its insertion is, that some Regiments, which have been long embodied, and are in the custom of assembling for permanent duty in quarters, have been in the practice of a regular evening parade of this description, with a view to maintain uniformity, and neatness of dress and appearance, as well as regularity and discipline while in quarters.

To Fire a Feu de Joie on Foot,

the Line is drawn up at Order with Arms advanced.

"*Commence firing on the Right.*" The right hand man of the front rank commences the fire, which will run down the front and up the rear, as quick as possible. When the right hand man of the rear rank has fired, the whole will glance their eyes to the right, to bring the carbine to the loading position, and when loaded they remain steady, waiting for the word.

"*Ready—Present.*" As before directed. The same to be repeated a third time; then after the third fire, "~~Half-cock Arms~~—*Advance Arms—Present Arms—Advance Arms.*"

Three cheers.

Section V. DUTIES OF SENTRIES.

Sentries are not to quit their arms, or walk more than ten yards on each side of their post; they are never to talk, loiter, or lounge, but are to move about briskly, in a soldier-like manner;—on the appearance of an Officer, they are to stand firm on any part of their walk, paying the compliment due, until the Officer has passed, taking care to front the same way they were posted. To all Field Officers, and to Officers of a superior rank, they present their arms; to all other Officers, they advance arms: all guards and sentinels must pay the same compliments to Officers of the Royal Navy and Marines as are directed to be paid to the Officers of the Army, according to their relative ranks. Although guards do not turn out after sunset to pay compliments, yet sentinels, whenever Officers approach their posts, must pay them a proper attention, by standing steady with carried arms, facing to their proper front; nor must this be left off until the evening is so far advanced, that they begin challenging.

On any one approaching his post, the sentry must challenge them by the words "*Who comes there?*" and at the same moment port arms. If the person approaching gives a satisfactory reply, the sentinel will direct him to pass.

Sentries posted with advanced arms may afterwards "support" them.

Corporals marching with reliefs are to be on the ~~left~~ *right*, and carry their arms advanced.

Section VI.

DIRECTIONS FOR FUNERAL PARTIES.

The party appointed for the escort, according to the rank of the deceased, is to be drawn up two deep, with open ranks, facing the place where the corpse is lodged; and when it is brought out, the Officer commanding will give the following words of command:

"*Present Arms.*" As in the Manual Exercise.

"*Reverse Arms.*" The right hand strikes the butt of the carbine, which is turned upwards; the guard turned towards the body; it is then placed under the left arm, seizing the cock and hammer with the left fore-fingers and thumb. The right hand is thrown behind the body, and grasps the carbine; the right heel at the same time is brought to its original position.

The Officers' swords are reversed under the right arm: the point of the sword downwards, grasping the hilt with the right hand.

"*Rear Rank, take Close Order.*" The ranks are closed, and the commands are then given to wheel by Threes or Divisions, so as to stand in column left in front.

When the procession is ready,

"*March.*" The party moves off in slow time, followed by the Band, playing the Dead March.

THE CORPSE.

PALL-BEARERS OF EQUAL RANK WITH THE DECEASED.

CHIEF MOURNERS.

OFFICERS TWO AND TWO,

According to rank, the juniors next to the body of the deceased.

When the first division of the funeral party arrives near the burial ground, the word of command, "*Halt*," is given, and the Officer commanding will order the front rank to place themselves on one side, and the rank on the other, facing inwards, forming a lane for the corpse to pass through.

"*Rest upon your Arms Reversed.*" The carbine is quitted by the right hand, and brought upright; the muzzle placed upon the toes of the left foot. The left hand open is placed upon the butt-end of the carbine.

The soldier's head leaning rather forward, the right hand is brought up to the forehead shading the eyes.

The corpse, &c., having passed through the lane, the word "*Attention*" is given, on which the soldiers raise their heads and drop their right arms by their sides.

The ranks are next formed as before.

"*Reverse Arms—March.*" The whole move in ordinary time and form in line facing the grave.

The command will then be given,

"*Rest upon your Arms reversed.*" After the performance of the Funeral Service, the following words of command are given:

"*Attention—Present Arms.*" By changing the hand on the butt, raising the carbine, turning it over with the right hand, and then holding it in the position of "Presented Arms," seizing it with the left hand at the swell.

"*Advance Arms.*" Three volleys are then fired in the air, and after the third volley, close the ranks, and return to quarters right in front, quick time.

In marching back, the Band is not to play, until the party is entirely clear of the burial ground.

Section VII.

BELTS, ARMS, ACCOUTREMENTS, AND SADDLERY.

The use of black leather belts is strongly recommended, in order to avoid the trouble and inconvenience of pipe-clay.

1. When girdles are worn, they should be sewed round the back of the jacket, and fastened in front, otherwise they will seldom be properly put on by the men. But the old light dragoon jacket, like the Horse Artillery, is the most convenient, being worn without any girdle.

2. Care must be taken that the pouch-belts are sufficiently long to enable the men to get their ammunition out easily.

3. Swivels for the fore-sling of the sword should be avoided; they continually give way, however strongly made, and the scabbard becoming reversed, the blade falls out between the horse's legs, and produces serious accidents.

4. Instead of a clasp for the front of the sword-belt, a strong plain buckle enables the men to put on the belt much more neatly and well.

5. The aftermost sling of the sword should be full twice as long as the fore sling, upon which the whole weight of the sword should hang, the after sling being merely to check the sword from swinging about and striking against the horse's stifle.

6. The scabbards, hilts, and blades of the swords are to be cleaned with bath-brick occasionally, but usually kept oiled.

7. The barrels of the carbines and pistols are on no account to be cleaned with any rough substance, which would take off the browning; but, when perfectly dry and clean, they must be polished with a little bees' wax.

8. The springs of the locks of the fire arms must be eased, by lowering the cocks. The locks must not be taken off for cleaning.

9. The brass mountings of the carbines and pistols, the buckles of the belts, and the shoulder and helmet or cap scales, are to be cleaned with a leather or buff stick, and finely powdered rotten-stone, made damp. (The rotten-stone may be purchased at any druggist's shop.) The ornaments on the cap or helmet should generally be taken off previously to being cleaned. When replaced, the ornaments must be well secured with pegs, through the staples. Shoulder-scales should be separated from the pads, previous to cleaning them, to prevent their being dirtied.

The buttons of the jackets, if tarnished, must be rubbed lightly with a piece of soft wash-leather, or a button-brush and whiting. Every man should provide himself with a button-stick.

10. The saddlery should be cleaned with soft soap; the bits, buckles, and stirrups should always be kept oiled, except when brightened for parade.

The men should be much cautioned to keep all saddlery in their houses when not wanted, as the damp of the stable has a much greater effect on leather when not in constant use than is usually supposed. All dirt or rust should be carefully rubbed off immediately on return from duty, though the men may not have time to clean them properly till later.

11. The saddles, bridles, and all the straps, must be sponged, and with soft soap perfectly divested of dirt and stains. The saddles and valise-pads should always after use be laid out in the sun, or before the fire, to dry the pannel, which should be beaten and brushed frequently to prevent its growing hard and full of lumps, by which the horse is injured, and the pannel rotted and destroyed.

12. The bits, stirrup-irons, and spurs, are to be polished with bath-brick, and made dry and free from rust; afterwards to be slightly rubbed over with sweet oil.

Section VIII.

MILITARY HORSEMANSHIP.

Accustoming the Horse to Arms and Firing.

1. Young horses must be very gradually accustomed to drawing and returning swords, the sword exercise, and firing, both before them and off their backs.

2. The horse, being naturally afraid of these things, must not have his terror added to by harsh treatment. By patience and gentleness he becomes familiar with them, and sees and hears them without alarm. One minute's loss of temper, or violence in the rider, may throw the horse back for a month.

3. In all practice with arms, at first, suddenness of movement should be avoided, and everything be done smoothly and quietly.

4. To use the horse to firing, a pistol flashed in the pan, for some days, and a little corn given to him after it; and then firing the pistol daily, giving a handful of corn after it, will generally succeed in making him quite steady with fire-arms.

5. A horse that is frightened at a feather or helmet should have one placed in his stable at a distance, and then, by bringing it a little nearer daily, he will at last allow it to be placed even in his manger without fear.

6. To accustom a horse to carrying a sword, a piece of stick, short and light, should first be hung from his back for several hours daily in the stable; a heavier one should then be tied on. Afterwards, a scabbard without the sword; when alarmed a few oats should be given in the hand. If the noise of the sword is what alarms him, the rings of the scabbard should for some days be tied round with packthread, to prevent their having any play, and making a noise.

Bridling.

1. Collar.—Placed so that the cheek-piece is parallel with, and behind, the cheek-bone of the horse. The upper edge of the nose-band two fingers' breadth from the point of the cheek-bone.

2. Headstall and Bridle.—Over the collar; the cheek-piece, parallel with the nose-band, passing through the squares of the collar; to be buckled so as to admit the finger to pass between it and the collar.

3. Bit.—To be placed straight in the horse's mouth, the bar one inch above the lower tusk, but so as to clear the upper tusks. Mares having no tusks, the bit must be placed about two inches above the corner tooth.

4. Bridoon.—Placed over the bit and fastened with the long end of the T (through the squares of the collar) in the keepers made for the purpose above them; it must fit easy without gagging, and the throat-band admit three fingers between it and the jaw-bone.

5. Curb-chain.—In fixing the curb-chain, care must be taken to turn the hand to the right until all the links are flat, then place the first link upon the hook, and afterwards the third and fourth link (as circumstances may require). When the curb-stone is properly fitted, one finger should be able to pass freely between it and the horse's jaw, the bit being held straight in the mouth.

Saddling.

1. Before putting the saddle on the horse's back, throw the girth, crupper, stirrup-irons, &c. over the seat of the saddle in order to prevent accidents, which too frequently occur from a horse being approached suddenly with these trappings loose.

2. The Saddle should at first be placed rather forward, gently drawing it back (to smooth the hair) to its place in the centre of the back. The front of the saddle should then be a hand's breadth behind the play of the horse's shoulder.

3. The crupper is next taken, care being observed that it is rather loose than tight, and placed under the horse's tail, with the hair cleared from under it. There should be room for the breadth of three fingers to pass freely between the crupper and the horse's croup.

4. Breast-plate.—To be placed in such a manner as to bring the lower part of the rosette (when the horse's head is raised) upon the point bone of the horse's chest, three fingers being allowed to pass underneath, as in cruppering.

5. Girth.—Should be passed through the lower part of the breast-plate, and not buckled tighter than to allow one finger to pass between it and the horse's side.

6. Shabracque.—Over the saddle.

7. Valise.—To be placed with the pocket uppermost and the buckles towards the saddle, outer baggage-straps well apart from the centre-strap, and their buckles rather between the cantle of the saddle and the valise. To accustom a young horse to the valise, it must at first be laid on very gently, and after he has had a good deal of exercise. It should only be lightly stuffed with hay for the first few times.

8. Surcingle.—Over all, placed neatly on the girth and not tighter than it.

Leading the Horse.

The reins of the snaffle being taken over the horse's head, are to be held with the right hand, the fore-finger between them, near the rings of the snaffle, the end or loop of the reins in the left hand, which hangs easy by the side.

When merely holding the horse, the reins need not be taken over his head, but both should be held behind the jaw with the fore-finger between them.

In leading his horse through a doorway, the man should always go before him sideways, looking back to see that he does not strike his hips, or catch any part of the saddlery against the door-post or latch.

Open Manège.

An open manège is formed by measuring out a piece of level ground about sixty yards long by twenty in width, with the corners marked, either by large stones or stakes; but if the latter, they should be at least six feet high, to prevent accidents.

The men lead their horses into the manège, and form in a line along one side, with a horse's length (eight feet) between each horse.

Mounting.

"*Stand to your Horses.*" The position of the man as in Foot Drill, but holding the left bridoon rein near the ring of the bit, with the right hand; toes in a line with the horse's fore feet; left hand hanging down by the thigh.

"*Prepare to Mount.*" [In Four Motions.] Face to the right on the left heel; place the right foot opposite the stirrup, heels six inches apart; take the bridoon rein, equally divided, in the left hand, and the bit reins in the right hand, placing the little finger of the left between them*, the left hand below the right on the neck of the horse, about twelve inches from the saddle.

"*Two.*" The right hand draws the reins through the left, and shortens them, so that the left has a light and equal feeling of both reins on the horse's mouth, the right hand remaining over the left.

"*Three.*" The right hand throws the reins to the off side, takes a lock of the mane, brings it through the left hand, and twists it round the left thumb; the left hand closes firmly on the mane and reins, the right hand quits the mane, and lays hold of the left stirrup.

---

* The bridoon is to be taken in the same manner as the bit reins when used singly.

"*Four.*" The left foot is raised and put into the stirrup, as far as the ball of it; the right hand is placed on the cantle, and the left knee against the saddle on the surcingle; the left heel is to be drawn back in order to avoid touching the horse's side with the toe.

"*Mount.*" [In Three Motions.] "*One.*" By a spring of the right foot from the instep rise in the stirrup, bring both heels together, knees firm against the saddle, heels drawn back a little, the body upright, and partly supported by the right hand.

"*Two.*" The right hand moves from the cantle to the pummel or off holster, and supports the body while the right leg passes clear over the horse; the right knee closes on the saddle, and the body comes gently into it.

"*Three.*" The left hand quits the mane, and the right the holster; the bridle hand takes its proper position; the right hand drops by the thigh.

The right foot takes the stirrup without the help of hand or eye. In Mounting with Carbine Slung, it must first be passed over the saddle, muzzle first, and downwards.

Dismounting.

"*Prepare to Dismount.*" [In Three Motions.] The right hand takes the rein above the left; the right foot quits the stirrup.

"*Two.*" The right hand holding the rein, the left slides forward upon it, about twelve inches from the saddle, feeling the horse's mouth very lightly.

"*Three.*" The right hand drops the reins to the off side, takes a lock of the mane, brings it through the left hand, and twists it round the thumb, the fingers of the left hand closing on it; the right hand is then placed on the holster.

"*Dismount.*" [In Four Motions.] Supporting the body with the right hand and left foot, the right leg is brought clear over to the near side; heels close; the right hand on the cantle preserves the balance of the body.

"*Two.*" The body is gently lowered until the right foot touches the ground.

"*Three.*" Resting on the right foot the left stirrup is quitted, and the left foot is placed in a line with the horse's hoofs; the hands remain as in the former motion.

"*Four.*" Both hands quit their hold; the man faces to the left, and brings the body square to the front; as he is turning, the right hand lays hold of the bridoon rein near the ring of the bit.

In preparing to dismount with a carbine, it is to be carefully passed behind the back to the near side, hanging by the swivel, muzzle downwards.

Position on Horseback.

The body balanced in the middle of the saddle; head upright and square to the front; shoulders well thrown back; chest advanced; upper part of the arms hanging down straight from the shoulders; left elbow bent and lightly closed to the hips; little fingers on a level with the elbow; wrist rounded, throwing the knuckles to the front.

The thigh stretched down from the hip; the flat of the thigh well turned inward to the saddle; knees a little bent; legs hanging straight down from the knee, and near the horse's sides; heels stretched down, the toes raised from the insteps, and as near the horse's sides as the heels.

Management of the Reins.

In riding with the bit, the bridoon rein to be held in the full of the bridle hand, passing under the middle joint of the thumb, and over the longest joint of the fore finger, the thumb closed firmly on the bit rein.

A formed horse may be rode on the bit entirely; but on first bitting the bridoon is to be used with both hands, in order to bring him to the bit by degrees.

At first the bit rein to be held loosely without feeling the mouth—the bridoon being only used as a snaffle. Afterwards, the bridoon rein is to be taken through the left hand into the right; and by feeling the bit gently with the bridle hand, the horse is to be made to step back, and encouraged when he obeys. Afterwards the bit alone may be used; but the right hand should for some time be ready to assist with the bridoon rein, if the horse is uneasy with the bit.

Where a horse continues fretful with the bit for a long time, the mouth-piece is most likely ill suited to him, and should, if possible, be changed; or it may proceed from his not having been sufficiently prepared with the snaffle; in which case the snaffle should be resumed, and the bitting put off a little longer.

The little finger of the bridle hand has four actions:

1. Towards the breast.

2. Towards the right shoulder.

3. Towards the left shoulder.

4. Towards the horse's head.

1. In "Halting," the little finger is turned upwards towards the breast.

In "Reining Back," the wrist is bent towards the body, and eased again alternately at every step.

In "Turning to the Right," and "Right About," the little finger is turned, and the hand a little raised towards the right shoulder.

In "Right Pass," the little finger towards the right shoulder. If the fore hand is too much advanced, the little finger towards the body to check it.

In "Working to the Left," the same movements towards the left shoulder, as laid down above towards the right.

Riding Lesson.*

To make the horse obedient in turning, reining back, &c., the bit rein should, in the first lessons, be held quite loose, and the man should take the bridoon rein, using both hands and keeping them about six inches apart†.

"*Eyes Right, March.*" In "moving forward," the little finger towards the horse's head to ease the reins for a moment.

"*Halt.*" In halting, a steady feeling of both reins by bringing the little fingers towards the breast, nails turned upwards; both legs closed for a moment to keep the horse up to the hand; hands eased as soon as halted.

"*Rein Back.*" A light feeling of both reins; little fingers towards the breast, and pressure of both legs to raise the fore hand, and keep the haunches under the horse; ease the reins after every step, and feel them again.

"*Right* (or *Left*) *Turn.*" A double feeling of the inward rein, the outward retaining a steady feeling.

The horse kept up to the hand, by a pressure of both legs, the outward leg the strongest, to keep the haunches from being thrown too much out.

"*Right* (or *Left*) *About.*" A double feeling of the inward rein, and stronger pressure of the inward leg, supported by the outward leg and rein, the horse turning on his centre.

OBSERVATIONS. By a turn-about the dressing is changed.

In turning to the right or right-about, the little finger of the right hand is to work towards the right shoulder; in turning left or left-about, the left little finger towards the left shoulder, upwards in both cases, to raise the fore hand.

In working to the right the thumb of the inward (right)

---

* This Instruction is given rather as a reference for those who have leisure to acquire the rudiments of military riding, than as a necessary practice for Yeomanry; and it should by no means supersede the Instruction in Squadron, even when occasionally practised.

† A horse which is unsteady in the ranks should at first be ridden with the snaffle in both hands, the man being allowed to return his sword.

MILITARY HORSEMANSHIP. 19

hand to be on a level with the little finger of the left: the inward rein an inch shorter, so as to let the rider see the horse's inward eye.

It must be well explained, that lightness of hand consists in an almost imperceptible feeling and alternate easing of the bridle, according to the motion of the horse, by which the delicacy of its mouth is preserved.

"*Dress.*" The two men on the flank being placed with their horses square, the remainder take up the dressing in succession from the flank to which the dressing is ordered, each keeping the same interval.

Bodies to be quite square to the front; heads well up, and just turned enough to allow a glance of the eye towards the dressing point, so as to see only the surface of the face of the next man but one. No attempt must be made to catch the dressing, by leaning forward or back.

When moving across the manège in Line, dressing must be correctly kept.

On arriving within a yard of the opposite side of the manège, each man, without any word of command, turns to the hand to which he dressed in marching, and moves along the side, keeping his horse's head at one yard distance from the croup of the horse in front of him.

OBSERVATIONS. The "Dressing" remains to the same hand till changed by

1. Turning about.
2. Inclining.
3. Passaging. All these operations change the dressing.

The above aids and directions should be gradually explained to the men as they make progress, and the Instructor must bear in mind, that to attempt to throw horses upon their haunches at once, which have not been early and regularly trained for Military riding, would only lame and injure them, and therefore too much exactness and squareness in the turns, or in reining back, must not be required.

"*Eyes Right—March—Right Turn.*" Turns to the right, to be repeated till some improvement is made.

While moving across the manège, "*Halt.*"

"*Rein Back,*" followed by "*Forward.*" Press the calves of both legs, yield the hand for an instant, then feel the reins again; on arriving at the side, turn to the right as before.

"*Right Turn;*" then while moving across, "*Halt.*"

"*Right about Turn.*" Each file turns on his own centre. The dressing is now changed to the left; and each file, on reaching the side, turns to the left, without word of command.

"*Left Turn.*" Repeated till well done.

"*Halt—Rein Back—Forward.*"

"*Left Turn.*"

"*Left about Turn.*"

This last turn changes the dressing to the right.

The squad should occasionally be halted by the side of the manège in file, and reined back a few steps.

When they have been worked at a walk till they preserve their dressing and make the turns well,

"*Trot.*" Ease the reins, and press the calves of both legs according to the horse's temper, then feel both reins to raise the fore hand.

The men must preserve the position and seat more by the balance of the body, than by clinging with the knees.

At a trot the body must be inclined a little back, the whole figure pliant, and accompanying the movements of the horse. The elbows and legs steady.

They should practise the turns at a trot the same as at a walk, to either hand; and should file down the centre, to make them keep a straight line and cover well.

In making use of spurs the man must be taught not to move his thighs or lean the body forward; the leg only should move, and the spur be applied just behind the girth.

The spur should be used as little as possible; but when it is, the horse should feel it; because a continued touching lightly with the spur will either make the horse kick, or cause him to become insensible to it.

"*Canter.*" A light and firm feeling of both reins, to raise the horse's fore hand; a pressure of both legs, to bring the haunches under him.

A double feeling of the inward rein, and a stronger pressure of the outward leg, to make the horse strike off true and united. The horses should lead off correctly, without throwing their haunches in; the rider, in applying the leg for cantering, is to remain steady in the middle of the saddle, without leaning forward. If a horse is false, the man should not check the ride, but close up to half the distance ordered, make a pause at the next corner, feel the inward rein, and close the outward leg, to make him change.

In going to the right, a horse should lead with the off fore foot, followed by the off hind: in going to the left, with the near fore followed by the near hind.

In cantering to the right, a horse leading with the two near legs is "false," and the reverse in cantering to the left.

Movements by Threes.

THE squad being formed at close files in single rank, three yards from the side of the manège, is told off by Threes from the right. The right hand man saying "*Right*," the next "*Centre*," the next "*Left*," the next "*Right*," &c. &c.

"*Threes Right.*" The Rights and Lefts of Threes cast their eyes to the Centres, who, at the last sound of the word, immediately begin turning their horses to the right, without moving either forward or backward.

The Rights rein back in a circular direction, closing the right legs to bring the croups round.

The Lefts move forward in a circular direction, closing the left legs to keep the haunches from flying out.

The squad being in column of Threes, right in front, each Three dressed correctly to the left, and the files covering, at the word

"*March*." The whole move forward, dressing to the (left) pivot hand. The pivot files are answerable for covering and keeping up to the same distance to the file before them, as when dressed after the wheel.

The leading pivot conducts the column, and is answerable for direction and pace.

Before changing direction at the corners of the manège, it must be explained that the pivot does not halt, but continues in motion, describing part of a circle into the new direction, while the others conform to the movement by a gradual change of direction and quickening their pace, taking care not to fly off from, or press on the pivot, and also not to lose the dressing.

"~~Leading Threes~~, *Left Wheel*." At this word, the Column commences the change of direction, and, when completed, at the word

"*Forward;*" the pivot moves straight to the front, the rest dressing and square.

This being repeated so as to round the two corners of the manège at each end, the squad arrives at its original ground.

"*Halt.*" The hand to be eased the instant the horse stops. Dressing of threes, and distances to be corrected, but not too exactly, as it renders the horses unsteady.

"*Front.*" The Centres turning their horses to the left, the Lefts reining back, the Rights moving forward in a circular direction, the whole come into line, and receive the word "*Left Dress.*"

The command "*Dress,*" includes exactness of the line, and correct interval between knee and knee, from the dressing hand.

"*Eyes Front.*" The men look straight before them, and all dressing and correction ceases; the hands to be eased immediately.

The same movements to be made to the left.

"*Threes Right—March.*" Then ordering a change of direction at the corners of the manège, by "~~Leading Threes,~~ *Left Wheel.*"

"*Halt—Left Incline.*" Each man turns his horse one-third to the left, on the horse's fore feet, so that each has his left knee behind the right knee of the man to the left of him. The whole dress to their left. They must, on no account, come before the left hand man, and must not press upon or fly off from him; each horse to move free and straight on his own line.

"*March.*" In a slanting direction across the manège.

When about half way across the manège,

"*Forward.*" Each man squares his horse, supporting with the left leg to keep the haunches from flying out, and the whole move forward, as before the incline took place.

"*Halt—Threes About.*"

It is to be explained that this is always right about. At the last sound of the word, the Centres turn right about; the Rights and Lefts conform, by continuing the same movements as in " Threes Right," till the wheel about is completed, when they halt and dress.

Wheel of Threes on the Move*.

It is to be explained, that (on the move), "*Threes Right*" being ordered, the Rights and Centres of Threes look to the left, and each Three commences wheeling as a Division on the fore feet of the horse of its Right, the Centres and Lefts both advancing and circling to the right till the wheel is completed; and at the word "*Forward*" the whole advance, each Three dressing to the left.

In the same manner (on the move), the "*Wheel About*" will be made by the Centres and Lefts wheeling forward and circling to the right, till the wheel about is completed, their horses bent to the right, and the left legs closed, to keep the haunches from flying out; every Right of Threes circling his horse's croup round on the fore feet by the pressure of his right leg.

---

* The method here laid down of wheeling the Threes on their flank men instead of on their Centres, is recommended to the Yeomanry for all occasions, because the trifling gain of a few feet towards the flank, which happens in consequence, is but a small inconvenience compared with the difficulty of reining back an imperfectly trained horse in a circular direction, as is requisite in wheeling Threes upon their Centres.

Section IX.

CARBINE EXERCISE ON FOOT.

As soon as the Recruit is sufficiently instructed in the Elementary Exercise of Marching, Facing, &c., he is to be taught the Exercise of the Carbine on Foot, and carefully instructed in all the details connected with Loading, and Firing with Ball, the whole of which are as necessary for the Cavalry as for the Infantry Soldier.

The Exercise of the Carbine on Horseback is to be commenced when the Recruit shall have made a sufficient progress in Horsemanship, as directed in the Instructions on Military Equitation.

Manual Exercise.

The Troop or Squad falls in for Drill, standing at Ease, with Carbine at the "Support;" that is, with the right hand brought forward and raised, holding the Carbine with the three last fingers under the cock, the thumb above, and the fore fingers under the guard, and about three inches below the bottom of the jacket; the arms to be kept near the body, the guard of the Carbine turned upwards, the swivel bar touching the hip, and the muzzle to the right rear; the left hand laid over the right, the left knee bent, and the right foot drawn back six inches.

"*Attention.*" Spring smartly up to the position of the "Advance," that is, with the Carbine perfectly upright against the side, the arm fully extended, the elbow close to the guard of the Carbine to the front; the thumb above the guard; the fore finger under it, and the other fingers under the cock.

"*Present Arms.*" The thumb of the right hand is placed under the cock; the Carbine is raised about two inches, and the muzzle is brought forward from the arm about four inches; at the same time the left hand is brought briskly across the body, and seizes the Carbine a little above the gripe.

"*Two.*" The right hand raises the Carbine, grasping the small of the stock; the left hand, quitting its position above the gripe, is placed above the lock, fingers round the stock, and the side of the hand resting on the guard; the point of the thumb as high as, and opposite to, the left eye; both elbows close.

"*Three.*" The Carbine is brought down to the extent of the right arm, the butt projecting, letting the barrel fall on the bend of the left; the lock turned a little outwards, and the cock resting against the knuckle joint of the first finger, this and the second finger only resting on the small of the stock, the others shut in the hand; the points of the first and middle finger of the left hand touching the swell of the stock in front of the lock; and the first finger close to the middle one, the others shut in the hand; the point of the thumb touching the seam in the centre of the flap of the trowsers; the right foot at the same instant drawn back about six inches behind the left heel; both knees straight.

"*Advance Arms.*" "Advance" the Carbine, steadying it with the fingers of the left hand, and bringing up the right foot.

"*Two.*" Drop the left hand to its place by the side.

"*Port Arms.*" At one motion throw the Carbine to a diagonal position across the body, the lock to be outwards, and at the height of the breast, the right hand grasping the small of the butt, just below the right breast; the left holding the Carbine at the gripe, the thumbs of both hands pointing towards the muzzle.

N.B. In this position the Carbine may be half-cocked at one motion, by the word "*Half-Cock Arms,*" for the purpose of inspecting the nipple, cock, &c., by placing the thumb of the right hand on the cock, and with the elbow well raised to the front, drawing back the cock to the catch of the half-cock. If the springs are to be eased, at the command "*Ease Springs,*" press the fore finger tightly on the trigger, draw the cock back with the thumb to the full cock, with an equal pressure on the trigger and cock; then lower it very carefully and gently on the nipple.

"*Advance Arms.*" Bring the Carbine down from the "Port" to the "Advance;" the left hand steadying it.

"*Two.*" Bring the left hand to its place by the side.

"*Support Arms.*" The right hand is brought forward and raised, retaining its hold of the Carbine as before directed.

"*Stand at Ease.*" The left hand is laid over the right, the left knee bent, and the right foot drawn back six inches.

Platoon Exercise.

"*Spring Arms.*" The Carbine is raised from the "Advance," by the right hand, as high as the hip, with the lock turned downwards, and is seized with the left at the gripe, the right hand seizing the swivel, and securing it through the ring; then grasp the small of the butt with the right hand.

"*Two.*" Bring the Carbine to the "Advance," and quit it with the left hand.

"*Load.*" Make a quarter face to the right; drawing the right foot back six inches, bring the left hand smartly across the body; grasp the Carbine a little above the gripe, and bring it down with the butt against the outside of the left leg and resting on the swivel, the barrel turned towards the front, the muzzle pointed forward and opposite to the middle of the chest, the right hand holding and steadying the muzzle*.

"*Handle Cartridge.*" Carry the hand to the pouch, take hold of a cartridge, draw it out, and bite off the end.

"*Two.*" Bring the right hand down to the muzzle; shake the powder into the barrel, put in the paper and the ball; and then take hold of the head of the ramrod with the fore finger and thumb.

---

* In this position, ramrods are sprung for inspection, or arms examined after firing.

"*Draw Ramrod.*" Draw out the ramrod and put it into the barrel, about six inches.

"*Ram Down Cartridge.*" Push the cartridge to the bottom.

"*Two.*" Strike it twice smartly with the ramrod.

"*Return Ramrod.*" Draw the ramrod out of the barrel, and return it into the pipe, forcing it well home; the fore finger and thumb still holding the ramrod.

"*Prime.*" Bring the Carbine to the "priming position" against the right side, the muzzle raised as high as the upper part of the peak of the cap or helmet, but pointing directly to the front; the left hand across the body holding the Carbine at the gripe, and the thumb a little above the swivel-bar; the thumb of the right hand placed upon the cock, the fingers behind the guard, half-cock the Carbine*, and then grasp the small of the butt.

"*Two.*" Carry the right hand to the cap pocket, take out a cap and place it on the nipple, the thumb pressing on the cap with the fingers shut.

"*Ready.*" Place the thumb of the right hand upon the cock, the fingers behind the guard; cock the Carbine, and grasp the small of the butt.

"*Present.*" Raise the Carbine steadily to the "Present," and look along the barrel; place the fore finger before the trigger, but avoid touching it, the Carbine well pressed to the shoulder by the three last fingers of the right hand.

"*Fire.*" By the action of the fingers alone, and by a gradual but firm pressure, pull the trigger and remain looking along the piece†.

Advance Arms." Bring the Carbine to the "Advance" and front, bringing the right foot up to the left.

---

* Here remove the old cap if there be one.

† To repeat the practice, at the word "Load," the Carbine may be brought at once from the shoulder to the loading position.

"*Trail Arms.*" Seize the Carbine a little above the gripe with the left hand to steady it, then with the right seize it at the gripe, drop it to the full extent of the arm, and quit it with the left hand, the barrel level, and the muzzle straight to the front.

"*Advance Arms.*" Come to the "Advance."

"*Unspring Arms.*" Raise the Carbine with the right hand as high as the hip, and seize it with the left at the "Gripe," (that is, with the full hand round the barrel and stock,) the lock downwards; the muzzle raised and in front of the chin; then "unspring" by disengaging the swivel from the Carbine, drop the swivel behind, and seize the small of the butt with the right hand.

"*Two.*" Bring the Carbine to the Advance and quit it with the left hand.

"*Support Arms.*"—"*Stand at Ease.*"

When the Instructor considers the Squad sufficiently expert in the exercise in slow time by numbers, he will cause it to be performed in quick time without numbers: by the words "*Load,*" "*Ready,*" "*Present,*" "*Fire.*" When fired, come at once to the loading position as before, and the firing is then continued by the words "*Ready,*" "*Present,*" "*Fire.*"

Care must be taken that the distinct motions are not confused by improper haste.

When a certain number of rounds are to be fired, the caution is given, "*Fire (—) Rounds, and Advance Arms.*"

From the priming position, the firing may be stopped by the words "*Advance Arms.*"

When the Ranks are doubled, the Rear-rank men, at the word "*Load*" or "*Ready,*" take a moderate pace to the right with their right feet, and when the Carbine is brought to the "Advance," resume their former position.

Blank Cartridge Firing.

The Recruit, in loading, is to be instructed to shake the powder well out of the cartridge, and to ram the paper, as wadding, home. The Instructor will then make each Recruit fire singly, looking to his levelling, and pay very particular attention that the cheek is not removed, nor must any start of the head be permitted.

When several Recruits are steady in their firing singly, they will be placed first in a single rank, that every man may be observed, and two or three men fire together by word of command; afterwards a couple of files will fire two deep, occasionally changing ranks; then the files will be increased by degrees, until the Squad fires together.

The Rear-rank men must be particularly attended to, as they generally fire too high; this is a great fault, and every soldier must be cautioned against it. The lower part of a man's body, at 150 yards, is the best general rule to lay down for aim.

Ball Firing.

The first target for the instruction of Recruits is to be round, and the practice will commence at a distance of thirty yards, so that it will be almost impossible that the Recruit should miss it. This method produces confidence in the young soldier at the commencement of his practice; for finding that he always hits at a certain distance, he feels encouraged for an increased range.

The range will be increased by degrees to 50—80—100 yards, at the same target; when the Recruits separately are steady at these distances, the Instructor will fire them by files, increasing the distance from fifty yards upwards, changing ranks occasionally, and then by the whole Squad.

The Recruit will now practise at a target of six feet by two, as the last of his drill. This target is divided by black lines into three compartments, Upper, Centre, and Lower divisions, (the Centre division having a bull's-eye of eight inches diameter in its centre, surrounded, at two inches distance, by a circle of an inch broad,) and is placed at a range of 80 yards, which distance is to be increased as improvement takes place, to 100 and 150 yards.

This division of the target is necessary, in order to correct any soldier's general line of fire, by referring to former practice reports where his shots have been inserted—as, for instance, "always fires low," &c. The reports must be correctly copied into a book kept by each Troop for the purpose, and signed by the Officer who superintended the practice, according to the following form:

Report of the Target Practice of Capt. . . . . . Troop, on the . . . Day of									
No.	Names.	Dist. yards.	Hits.			Total Hits.	Total Misses.	Number of Rounds.	Remarks.
			Upper.	Centre.	Lower.				
1	Serjeant J. Adam	100	1	–	2	3	3	6	
2	Corporal B. Brown	..	–	×1	3	4	2	6	× Outer Circle.
3	Drum. C. Grant	–	2	°1	–	3	3	6	° Bull's Eye.
4	Private A. Alexander	–	–	–	–	–	–	–	In Hospital.
	Total	–	3	2	5	10	8	18	

(Signed)   J. D., Captain.

Section X.

CARBINE EXERCISE ON HORSEBACK.

1. When the Recruit has attained a degree of proficiency on foot, the Exercise of the Carbine on Horseback should often form a part of each riding-lesson.

2. The following instructions are given in detail as they are to be taught to Recruits in small Squads; but, as soon as they are perfect, they may proceed with the execution of the several commands without loss of time; and afterwards the Recruit may fire blank cartridge.

3. In the first lessons of the Recruit with the Carbine on Horseback, great care must be taken, that, in presenting to the front or left, he does not strike or touch the horse's head with the Carbine.

4. In Loading, he must be taught to shake the powder out of the paper into the barrel before he puts in the wadding; and when loading with Ball, to double the paper round it, so that it may require a small degree of force to drive it home; otherwise, when he "Slings" or "Straps" his Carbine, after it is loaded, the ball is apt to fall out.

5. In Priming, the Recruit must be made to understand that the cap when placed on the nipple should be well pressed down with the thumb, so that there may be no danger of its falling off.

6. In all the motions connected with firing, great care must be taken to avoid altering the accustomed feeling of the bridle in the horse's mouth, or the usual seat and balance of the man, and position of his legs, as tending to alarm the animal; for a horse once rendered timid by an accident in firing from his back, will make the practice of it both difficult and dangerous.

7. When the Recruit is familiar with the firings at the halt, he is to practise them while his horse is in motion; afterwards he must be taught to fire with ball at a suitable object, first at the halt, and afterwards when in motion.

To perform the exercise on horseback, the Squad is to be formed in one rank, with two yards from knee to knee.

"*Spring Arms.*" Take off the right hand glove, place it in the waist-belt; swivel and unstrap the Carbine; take off the lock-cover, secure it to the stay or Carbine-strap, and seize the Carbine with the right hand at the gripe.

"*Two.*" Draw the Carbine from the bucket, and, continuing to grasp it in the full hand, bring it to the "Advance," resting the hand upon the thigh; the barrel diagonally across the body; the muzzle a little elevated to the left front.

In this position the Carbine is carried by small detachments and advanced parties or videttes, being that from which the soldier most readily prepares to fire, and which occasions the least fatigue.

"*Load.*" Raise the Carbine in front of the face, pass the butt over to the left under the bridle arm, and lower it till it rests on the swivel, taking hold of it with the left hand to steady it in loading; the right hand holding and steadying the muzzle. In this position the bridle-hand must not be raised or disturbed.

"*Handle Cartridge.*" Carry the hand to the pouch, take hold of a cartridge, draw it out and bite off the end.

"*Two.*" Bring the right hand down to the muzzle. Shake the powder into the barrel, then put in the paper, or ball, and lay hold of the ramrod with the fore finger and thumb.

"*Draw Ramrod.*" Draw out the ramrod, and put it into the barrel about six inches.

"*Ram down Cartridge.*" Push the cartridge to the bottom.

"*Two.*" Strike it twice smartly with the ramrod.

"*Return Ramrod.*" Draw the ramrod out of the barrel, and return it into the pipe, forcing it well home, the fore finger and thumb still holding the end of the ramrod.

"*Prime.*" Change the right hand to the gripe (below the left) and raise the Carbine, keeping the muzzle well to the front,

CARBINE EXERCISE ON HORSEBACK.

letting go the left, and continuing to raise the piece with the right till you can pass the butt over to the off side; lay the Carbine in the left hand, and half-cock*. Then grasp the small of the butt with the right hand. This is called the Priming Position.

"*Two.*" Carry the right hand to the cap pocket; take out a cap and place it on the nipple, the thumb pressing on the cap with the fingers shut†.

"*Ready.*" Cock; then seize the small of the butt with the right hand.

"*Front Present.*" Raise the Carbine to the "Present" with both hands, and place the butt firmly against the hollow of the right shoulder; lean the head in order to take a steady aim; but the body must be upright. In raising the Carbine to the "Present," the greatest care must be taken not to disturb the feeling of the bridle in the horse's mouth; the motions must be made as smoothly and quietly as possible; and the reins may be a little lengthened.

"*Fire.*" Pull the trigger, still keeping the Carbine at the "Present," and the eye fixed on the object.

"*Load.*" Lower the butt of the Carbine and bring it down into the loading position. The remainder of the loading motions as before.

N.B. Preparatory to firing to the left, the horses must be turned to the right, in order to avoid accidents.

"*Ready.*" As before.

"*Left Present.*" Raise the Carbine to the "Present" to the left with the right hand; and in order to steady it, rest the barrel on the left arm, near the elbow, which for this purpose is to be raised almost as high as the shoulder.

"*Fire.*" As before.

---

* Remove the old cap, if there be one.
† From this position the arms may be advanced if not required to fire.

"*Advance Arms.*" As before.

N.B. The exercise should next be gone through in quick time, without numbers, as on foot.

From the "Advance" the Carbine may be carried or slung.

"*Carry Arms.*" Without altering the position and grasp of the right hand, raise the Carbine, and place the butt of it in the hollow of the thigh, where the hand previously rested; the muzzle to be carried to the front, so as to be in a line, clear of the horse's neck, and leaning rather forward; the elbow near the side. In this position the Carbine is carried by the "Advance Guard" in marches of parade.

"*Sling Arms.*" This position is taken from any of the preceding, by gently dropping the Carbine with the muzzle downwards behind the thigh, and leaving it "Slung," or suspended by the swivel only.

From being "Slung," the Carbine may be brought at once to any of the foregoing positions, or may be "Strapped."

"*Strap Arms.*" Seize the Carbine at the gripe, and lay it in the left hand; put on the lock-cover; then place the muzzle in the bucket; strap and unspring the Carbine, and drop the swivel; put on the right-hand glove, and let both hands resume their usual position.

Section XI.

PISTOL EXERCISE ON HORSEBACK.

The Squad is to be formed as for the Carbine Exercise.

"*Draw Pistol.*" Take off the right-hand glove, unbutton the flounce, and push forward the cloak, or draw back the sheepskin and shabraque, according to the equipment, and passing the right hand under the left arm, seize the butt of the Pistol.

"*Two.*" Draw the Pistol carefully, and bring it at once to the position in which the sword is "Carried," the muzzle a little to the front, the cock resting in the hollow between the thumb and the hand, the lower fingers relaxed and extended along the butt. This position is called the "Advance."

"*Load, &c.*" The several motions are to be made as directed for the carbine.

"*Front Present.*" Raise the Pistol, till the breach be nearly as high as, and in a line with, the right eye, with the muzzle lowered to the object; the hand lightly grasping the butt, the arm a little bent, and without stiffness, in order to keep the Pistol more correctly to its aim.

"*Fire—Load.*" As before.

Preparatory to firing to the right or left, the Squad must turn their horses, as directed in firing to a flank with the carbine.

"*Ready.*" As before.

"*Left Present.*" Resting the barrel on the left arm, as before directed for the carbine.

"*Fire—Load.*" As before.

"*Right Present.*" The Pistol is carried to the right, and raised and levelled as directed in presenting to the front.

"*Fire—Load.*" As before.

"*Rear Present.*" Carry the Pistol as far towards the rear as the body, turned from the hips only, will admit; take the aim and hold the Pistol in the same manner as directed for presenting to the front.

"*Fire, &c.*" As before. Half cock, and

"*Return Pistol.*" Drop the muzzle under the bridle arm, and place the Pistol carefully in the holster.

"*Two.*" Bring the right hand to its position by the thigh.

Section XII.

SWORD EXERCISE.

The instructions here given, although they must at first be explained and put in practice on foot, yet are only intended to prepare the men for the mounted exercise, and in executing both the Cuts and Guards, the supposed situation of the horse's head, and also the position of the man on horseback, must always be considered. For this reason the men must, in doing the exercise on foot, turn, bend, or stoop, from the hips only, without twisting the legs and feet.

In giving Cuts it must be explained that the effective part of the blade is about six inches from the point; and in making Guards, the most defensive part of the blade to oppose to an adversary is the half nearest the hilt.

The Sword should be held easy and flexible in the hand, as no strength is gained by too stiff a grasp.

In all Cuts and Guards the middle knuckles should be in the same direction as the edge.

In Cutting and Thrusting the motion should gradually increase in rapidity, so as to give the whole strength at the last. On horseback very little force is required for thrusting in the same direction as the horse is moving; and it is of the utmost consequence in that, as in every part of the exercise, that the man should not overreach himself, or alter the proper position of his legs by the horse's sides. Above all, it must be avoided to

SWORD EXERCISE.

stick out the leg on the opposite side from which he gives his Cut or Thrust; if anything, that knee should be more bent, and the foot more close to the horse.

Preparatory Instructions.

For preparatory instruction on foot, the men should be formed by Squads of eight or ten, in single rank, with three paces interval from man to man; the heels about a foot asunder.

"*Draw Swords.*" Bring the right hand across the body, over the bridle arm, which should be placed as if holding the reins; take the sword-knot, slip it over the wrist, and give the hand a couple of turns inwards, in order to make it fast, and at the same time seize the hilt, turning it to the rear, and raise the hand to the height of the elbow, the arm being close to the body. By a second motion draw the Sword smoothly from the scabbard, the hand raised till the point clears the scabbard, the edge being to the rear, and sink the hand till the hilt is in front of the chin, the blade upright, the edge to the left, and the elbow close to the body, which forms the position of "Recover Swords." By a third motion bring the hilt down on a level with the bridle-hand, the elbow near the body, the blade upright, the wrist slightly rounded, so as to turn the edge rather inwards. This is the position of "Carry Swords."

"*Slope Swords.*" Loosen the grasp of the handle, and let the back of the sword fall lightly on the shoulder, the wrist a little bent upwards.

"*Carry Swords.*" Grasp the handle so as to bring the blade upright.

"*Return Swords.*" Carry the hilt to the hollow of the left shoulder, the blade kept upright, and the back of the hand to the front; then by a turn of the wrist drop the point, and put it into the scabbard, turning the edge to the front, the hand and elbow square across the body. Then let the Sword fall smoothly into the scabbard, at the same time loosening the sword-knot, and withdrawing the hand.

In returning Swords the point is easier inserted by resting the blade upon the bridle arm; care should be taken that the Sword is not returned with force, but the edge preserved, by letting it fall gradually, with the back alone bearing against the scabbard.

"*Draw Swords.*" As before explained.

"*Right, prove Distance.*" "Recover the Sword" with the fore finger and thumb stretched along the handle; the thumb on the back, the end of the hilt in the palm of the hand. By a second motion, extend the sword to the right, the hand on a level with the shoulder, the edge to the rear.

In this, and throughout the instructions, where a second motion is required, the word of command "*Two*" must be given, unless the practice is carrying on with a Flugelman.

"*Slope Swords.*" As before.

"*Front, prove Distance.*" Raise the Sword to the "Recover" as before, then lean forward, and extend the point of the Sword, with the edge to the right.

"*Slope Swords.*" As before.

"*Engage.*" Bend the body with the chest drawn in, and bring the end of the sword-hilt to the pit of the stomach, the edge to the left, and point advanced.

"*Right Guard.*" Carry the Sword to the right, with the edge inclining to the rear, the point being advanced, and the arm remaining bent, with knuckles upwards.

"*Left Guard.*" Raise the arm, and carry the Sword to the left, with the point downwards, the edge and point rather to rear, the wrist being above, and in advance of, the peak of the cap.

"*Cut One.*" Extend the arm and raise the Sword above the right shoulder, the edge to the rear, and point downwards.

"*One.*" Cut low from front to rear on the left (or near) side, and continue the sweep of the Sword until the position of the arm is resumed ready to repeat the same Cut, and which

SWORD EXERCISE. 39

should be repeated (if requisite) by the word of command "*One*" as often as the Instructor deems it necessary, according to the proficiency of the men under instruction; the same rule to be followed with all the Cuts, from One to Six.

"*Cut Two.*" Turn the head to the right, and lower the Sword until the back touches the neck just above the left shoulder, the point being downwards to the rear, and the hand just above the left ear.

"*Two.*" Cut low from front to rear on the right (or off) side, continuing the sweep of the Sword, &c. as in the previous directions for "One."

"*Cut Three.*" Extend the arm to the rear, with the Sword perpendicular, and edge to the rear, the wrist being as high as the shoulder.

"*Three.*" Cut low from rear to front on the right, &c.

"*Cut Four.*" Turn the head and body to the left, bringing the hand into the hollow of the left shoulder, the point of the Sword being kept up, and the back lightly touching the neck, with the edge to the rear.

"*Four.*" Cut low from rear to front on the left side, &c.

"*Cut Five.*" Raise the hand, and extend the arm to the right, as high as the shoulder; the back of the Sword touching the neck, the edge to the rear, and knuckles downwards.

"*Five.*" Cut in a horizontal direction to the left, &c.

"*Cut Six.*" Turn the head to the right, and bending the arm, bring the Sword over the left shoulder, the back touching the neck with the point to the rear, and knuckles upwards.

"*Six.*" Cut horizontally direct to the right, &c.

"*Cut Seven.*" Raise the arm, with the hand in front, rather above the height of the head, the edge of the Sword upwards, and the point lowered to the rear of the right shoulder.

"*Seven.*" Cut downwards to the front, and remain with the arm extended, the hand in line with the shoulder, and thumb along the back of the handle.

"*First Point.*" Turn the edge of the Sword upwards to the right, and by raising the elbow, draw in the wrist just above, and in front of, the right eye, the point directed towards the left front.

"*Two.*" Deliver the point to the full extent of the arm, and bend the body, continuing to look under the wrist.

"*Second Point.*" Turn the knuckles downwards, the edge of the Sword upwards, and the thumb round the handle, drawing in the elbow until the wrist is just above the bridle hand, the point being to the right front.

"*Two.*" Deliver the point, raising the wrist as high as the head, and looking over the arm.

"*Third Point.*" Turn the knuckles and edge of the Sword upwards to the right, drawing in the wrist to the side, until it touches the upper part of the hip, with the point to the front.

"*Two.*" Deliver the point, and, as the wrist rises, look under the arm.

"*Slope Swords.*" As before.

The Seven Cuts are now combined, as also the Three Points, (preparing for the Cut "One" at the word of command "*Assault,*") and given at the words "*One,*" "*Two,*" respectively, and so on to "*Seven;*" and for the Points, the words "*First,*" "*Second,*" "*Third.*" In this practice, as each Cut is delivered, the Sword is brought up ready for the succeeding one, but after "Seven," preparing for the "First" Point, and following the same rule (after delivering the Point) in preparing for the "Second;" then the "Third;" and after the Third Point is given, the arm remains extended until the following word of command.

"*Right Defend.*" Turn the head and body to the right, bending the elbow until the hand is brought towards the shoulder, in advance of the face, with the point raised, and inclining to the rear, and edge to the front,—which forms "First Guard," so as to defend the face against Cut One.

"*Second Guard.*" Turn the edge to the rear, the point inclining to the front, and carrying the Sword to the rear, as high as the shoulder, so as to defend the face against Cut Two.

"*Third Guard.*" Turn the knuckles downwards, and lower the Sword to the full extent of the arm, with the edge to the front, and point to the rear, so as to defend the leg against Cut Three.

"*Fourth Guard.*" Turn the knuckles outwards, and edge to the rear, with the point to the front, so as to defend the leg against the Cut Four.

"*Fifth Guard.*" Turn the knuckles inwards, and raise the wrist to the front, as high as the shoulder, by bending the arm until the hand is on a line with the elbow, so as to defend the body against Cut Five.

"*Sixth Guard.*" Turn the edge of the Sword and arm to the rear, so as to defend the body against Cut Six.

"*Seventh Guard.*" Raise the elbow and hand above, and in advance of, the head, in line with the right shoulder, the edge upwards, and point rather downwards to the front, so as to defend the head against Cut Seven.

"*Parry.*" Lower the wrist towards the shoulder, and raise the point of the Sword with the edge to the rear; then, by a second motion, turn the wrist and arm so that the point forms a circle from front to rear, returning to its original position.

"*Left Defend.*" Form the "First Guard" on the left; the remaining Guards and Parry being now formed respectively on the left side, and by the same words of command as before on the right, and the preceding Instructions are equally applicable, excepting the words Front and Rear, which, of course, become reversed, in consequence of the body being turned to the left.

"*Slope Swords.*" As usual.

A successive combination of the Cuts and Points, so arranged as to show where they can be most effective against Cavalry or Infantry, is now shown in the two following Practice Divisions.

First Division.

"*Assault.*" Prepare for Cut One.

"*One.*" Cut One, and prepare for the First Point downwards on the left.

"*Point.*" Give the Point smartly downwards to the full extent of the arm, and immediately prepare for Cut Two.

The remaining Cuts are now given by their respective words of command, the Point following each Cut, and delivered in the same direction.

Second Division.

The same words of command as in the preceding Division, but the Point is now to be given on the reverse side to that on which the Cut has been previously made, excepting after the Cut Seven, when it is to be the Second Point, and given to the rear.

Review or Sword Exercise Mounted.

At a Review, the Sword Exercise is to be performed with Flugelmen, one in front of each flank, at about sixty yards' distance from the Line. The Commanding Officer gives the following words of command: "*Prepare for Sword Exercise,*" "*Single Files from the Right of Threes.*"

"*March,*" followed by "*Halt,*" as soon as the Threes are all in file. The Squadrons then correct their dressing by the centre of each, the Flugelmen take their posts, and the Officers move out as at "Order."

SWORD EXERCISE.

Words of Command.	Flugelman.
"*Right Prove Distance*"	Right.
"*Slope Swords*"	Right.
"*Front Prove Distance*"	Right.
"*Slope Swords*"	Right.
"*Engage*"	Right.
"*Right Guard*"	Right.
"*Left Guard*"	Right.
"*Assault*" (seven Cuts and three Points)	Left and Right.
"*Right Defend*" (seven Guards and Parry)	Right.
"*Left Defend*" (Ditto)	Right and Left.
"*Slope Swords*"	Left.

First Division.		Second Division.	
"*Assault*"	Right.	"*Assault*"	Right.
"*One*"	Left.	"*One*"	Left.
"*Point*"	Left.	"*Point*"	Right.
"*Two*"	Right.	"*Two*"	Right.
"*Point*"	Right.	"*Point*"	Left.
"*Three*"	Right.	"*Three*"	Right.
"*Point*"	Right.	"*Point*"	Left.
"*Four*"	Left.	"*Four*"	Left.
"*Point*"	Left.	"*Point*"	Right.
"*Five*"	Left.	"*Five*"	Left.
"*Point*"	Left.	"*Point*"	Right.
"*Six*"	Right.	"*Six*"	Right.
"*Point*"	Right.	"*Point*"	Left.
"*Seven*"	Right.	"*Seven*"	Right.
"*Point*"	Right.	"*Point*"	Rear.
"*Slope Swords*"	Right.	"*Slope Swords*"	Rear.

"*Front form Ranks.*" The Line is reformed by the Centres and Lefts dressing up to the Right of Threes, and the rear rank then closing up to their proper distance. Officers take their usual posts, and dress.

Section XIII.

OFFICERS' SALUTE, &c.

Salute Mounted.

Being at the position of "Carry Swords," raise the hand by a circular motion to the "Recover Swords," with the thumb extended on the side of the handle; then, without any pause, incline the hand to the right shoulder, and gradually lower the wrist to the right of the thigh, below the hip, with the elbow in, and Sword lowered until on a line with the knee, the point in the same direction as the foot, and the edge still kept to the left.

"Recover Swords," and instantly return to "Carry Swords."

The effect of the salute depends upon the manner and address with which it is given, and also upon properly observing the time, so that the movement may be uniform.

On Foot.

From the position of "Recover," bring the Sword slanting across the body to the "Port," with the edge downwards, and, by bending the left elbow, raise the hand as high as the shoulder, and take hold of the blade between the thumb and fore finger, the knuckles being to the front, and the thumb extended towards the point of the Sword.

The "Salute" is to be made from the "Recover," in the same manner as when mounted, the left arm being closed to the side as the Sword is raised to the "Recover."

PART THE SECOND.

INSTRUCTION OF THE TROOP AND SQUADRON.

PART THE SECOND.

Section I.

TERMS OF FORMATION AND MANŒUVRE.

A Rank, is any number of men side by side in line.

Cavalry are said to be marching by:

Files. When each front-rank man has his rear-rank man by his side, being a column two abreast.

Single File. When each front-rank man has his rear-rank man following behind him, the whole being thus in one single string.

Threes. When each front-rank "Three" has its rear-rank "Three" by its side, being a column six abreast.

Sections of Threes. When each front-rank "Three" has its rear-rank "Three" following behind it, being a column three abreast.

A Division, is the fourth part of a Squadron. Divisions are numbered 1st, 2nd, 3rd, and 4th from the right.

A Troop, is the half of a Squadron. Troops are Right and Left in each Squadron.

A Squadron. Two or more Squadrons compose a Corps or Regiment. Squadrons are called 1st, 2nd, 3rd, &c., counting from the right.

Distance, is the term used to denote the space from front to rear.

Interval, denotes the space from side to side.

Close Order. The ordinary distance at which the rear rank is formed behind the front rank.

Order. The increased distance taken by the rear rank on some occasions of parade.

Front. The direction towards which the Line or Column is facing, the rear being exactly the contrary direction*.

Point of Formation. Any fixed object or Marker upon which a body of Troops is directed to commence its formation into line.

Base. Two persons placed a short distance apart to mark the direction in which a Line or Column is to form.

The Base Squadron, Troop, or Division, is the one upon which a Formation is made.

Change of Front, is when the Line throws forward or retires either of its flanks, or throws forward one and retires the other, upon a Base Troop which merely wheels without leaving its ground.

Change of Position, is when the Line moves altogether off its ground, advancing or retiring one of its flanks.

Inversion. A Regiment is said to be inverted when the Squadrons are not in their proper order, but the Right Squadron on the left, and the Left on the right, as for instance, when the Squadrons entire have wheeled to the right or left about.

Column, is when the line is broken into several parts, each following exactly behind the other.

Direct Echellon, is when the line is broken into several parts, moving direct to the front or rear in this manner:

---

* It should be recollected that, whenever in a word of command mention is made of the Front or Rear, it means the front or rear of the Troops as then standing, without any reference to the ground, or to any former position.

48 TERMS.

Oblique Echellon, is when the Line is broken into several parts by half or quarter wheels from Line, or Column, so as to be oblique to the former front, and parallel with each other, thus:

/ / /

Alignment. A straight line upon which a body of Troops is to march or form.

Pivot. The outward man on the flank of a Squadron or smaller body upon which that body turns in wheeling.

The Pivot Flank, in column, is that which is the directing hand, and which, when wheeled up to, preserves each part of the line in its natural order; the other is called the Reverse Flank. Therefore, in all cases when the right is in front, the left is the pivot, and *vice versâ*.

Moveable Pivot, is when the flank man, during a wheel, makes a small sweep, instead of standing fixed.

Section II.

DISTANCES AND INTERVALS.

Distances.

1. From one horse to another when marching in file—One yard.

2. From front rank to rear rank at close order—Half a horse's length (four feet).

3. From front rank to rear rank at "Order" in line—Four horses' lengths.

4. From front rank to rear rank when marching past in Open Column—One fourth of the extent of front; in no case, however, exceeding twelve yards.

DISTANCES AND INTERVALS. 49

5. From one Squadron to another in Close Column—Two horses' lengths.

6. From one Squadron, Troop, or Division, to another in Open Column—The extent of front of each Squadron, Troop, or Division; this distance is taken from front rank to front rank; the leading Squadron, Troop, or Division allowing a Squadron interval in addition.

7. The depth of two ranks, taking the length of the full-sized cavalry horse at eight feet, and the distance between ranks at four feet, is to be reckoned at about twenty feet.

Intervals.

1. Between Files when formed in Squadron—Six inches from knee to knee.

2. Between Squadrons in line—The fourth part of the front of a Squadron.

3. The extent of Front of a Squadron is to be calculated at about as many yards as it contains Files.

Section III.

DIRECTIONS FOR INSTRUCTORS.

1. The first drills should be in small Squads in single rank, not exceeding twelve men in each. All general directions and explanations should be short and clear; the repetition of them, after they have been understood, should be avoided. Strict silence must always be required in the ranks.

2. At the drills, due allowance must always be made for young, unsteady, or violent horses. If the men are blamed for their horses' faults, they become impatient with them, and confirm them in their bad habits, which by gentleness, and by not requiring too much exactness of movement from them at first,

can almost always be overcome. If a horse is violent, the rider should always be allowed to return his sword, and ride with the snaffle in both hands at ordinary drills.

3. Short halts* should take place at intervals, the order being given to sit at ease; the men should also be dismounted at least once during the drill. The soldier whose attention is not fatigued will take the greater pains, and make the more rapid progress in consequence.

OBSERVATION. To avoid the loss of valuable time while Yeomanry are assembling, it is recommended that as the men arrive they should be formed (without any telling off) in Squads of from eight to twelve, and exercised by the Officers and Serjeants present in wheeling and inclining, until a quarter of an hour after the time fixed for Parade. After that they should fall in and proceed to the Roll-call and Formation, and Telling off of the Troop and Squadron.

Section IV. DRESSING.

DRESSING is a progressive operation upon two men placed in a determined straight line, by which any number of men are correctly aligned on them.

1. The first and second men on the standing flank being first truly placed, the others then rapidly and successively conform to them; and the men must be habituated to line themselves on the given points, without assistance or being called to.

2. The first principle of dressing, either halted or in movement, is the perfect squareness of the man and horse. The next is, that each man should see the surface, but no more, of the second man's face from him. To do this, he must sit upright on his horse, and not gain the line by leaning backward or forward.

---

* Nothing requires more attention than to impress on the men the advantage of easing the hand the instant after halting, in order to make the horses remain steady.

DRESSING.

The head must be kept square to the front, the glance of the eye only should secure the dressing.

3. During the dressing, the proper distance from knee to knee must be corrected.

4. The word "*Dress*" means to the hand to which the men are then looking; but when the dressing is to be to a different point, it will be expressed by the word "*Eyes Right*," "*Eyes Centre*," or "*Eyes Left*."

5. The Squadron and all other bodies, till otherwise ordered, dress to the hand to which they form, except in a Formation to the pivot hand, after a flank movement by Files or Threes, when the dressing is to the leading flank*. As soon as a Squadron is formed in line, the eyes are to the centre.

6. When the dressing is finished, the word "*Eyes Front*" is given.

7. On the march, dressing is to the hand to which it was when halted, or to that which becomes the pivot, or directing hand; and it is a rule, that when the right is in front, the left is the pivot or point of dressing and covering, and *vice versâ*.

8. On the halt, dressing is to the same hand as it was on the march.

9. In the formations from Threes and Files to the left (pivot) hand, the dressing does not alter to the right till each Three or File is actually arriving at those already formed; but in Formations to the Front, or Reverse Flank, the dressing changes to that Flank on the caution to "Form."

10. In Formations from Column of Divisions or Troops to the Reverse Flank, the dressing changes at the caution, and Troop Leaders shift accordingly.

11. When the Squadron moves in line, dressing is to its centre.

---

* For instance, when Threes are fronted after marching to a flank.

Section V.

MARCHING TO THE FRONT.

1. One of the most necessary instructions for preparing the soldier to act in Squadron is the method of marching perfectly straight, by keeping in one line two objects, such as tufts of grass, or stones, at some distance before him (see fig. 1); and for this purpose each man is to be successively placed on the directing hand; but at first a well-trained man must be placed there for this practice.

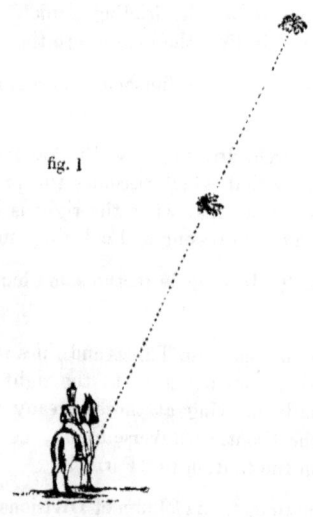

fig. 1

2. On the words "*Eyes Right, March,*" the whole move forward. The flank man must be cautioned never to move with suddenness or hurry, and the steadiness of his pace must be greatly attended to. The men must be taught to correct the distance from knee to knee as gently and quietly as possible, and much more by the leg than by the hand. Gradual correction of dressing and distance is the chief principle of good movement.

MARCHING TO THE FRONT.

3. The points of direction must be occasionally changed to the right or left (see fig. 2), to teach the men to close towards, or yield from, the pivot hand, it being a general rule to give way to any pressure from that flank, but to resist it from the other.

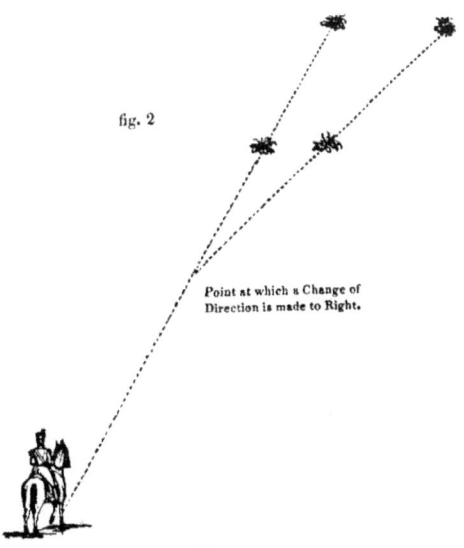

fig. 2

Point at which a Change of Direction is made to Right.

4. The Instructor must sometimes direct the flank man, in a low voice, to go faster or slower, observing that the rank conform in their dressing without suddenness or hurry.

5. After the "*Halt*" the men are to ease their hands and remain steady; if the word "*Dress*" follows, they quickly take up their line from the flank to which they are to dress. And to instil the practice of dressing, as it is generally necessary in manœuvre, the two men of a Squad on either flank are directed to advance a horse's length; and at the words "*Eyes Right* (or *Left*) *Dress*," each man successively dresses on these points. Dressing back must be practised exactly in the same manner, by causing the two men on the flank to rein back a little.

Section VI. INCLINING.

1. At the order to "Incline," each man causes his horse to turn on his fore feet, about one-third towards the flank, so that his knee comes rather behind the knee of his next leading file; and the whole will look to the hand to which they are to incline. The rear rank moves in the same manner, and is regulated by the front rank, which it takes care to conform to; and thus the horses' heads of the rear rank will be directed in rear of the second man from their leader towards the hand to which the "Incline" is made.

2. The Non-commissioned Officer (Guide) on the leading flank, having ascertained his points, marches steadily upon them, at whatever place is ordered. Every other man moves on so many parallel lines with respect to him, and preserves the same uniformity of front and files as when he first turned his horse's head, taking care that his horse does not slide or cross his legs, but moves quite straight.

3. Great care is to be taken that the whole move at the same pace, and quicken or slacken together, as ordered. If the flank that follows is too forward, the centre will be crowded; if it is too backward, the men will be too much in file.

4. Whenever the word "*Forward*" is given, each man, at the same instant, turns his horse to the front, and moves onward in the former direction.

Section VII.

PASSAGING AND REINING BACK.

When ground is to be taken to the flank by passaging, the whole move at the word "*Right* (or *Left*) *Pass*," "*March*," until the word "*Halt*." The horses must never be hurried, but made to passage very slowly, and for a very short space at a time.

In reining back, the whole look to the hand to which they ought to form or dress; the movement is never to be hurried, and the horses are to be kept straight by the pressure of the leg. A dead pull at the mouth must be avoided, the bridle being alternately eased and tightened as the horse steps backward.

Section VIII. WHEELING.

The following table shows the different degrees of wheeling, and the words of command for each.

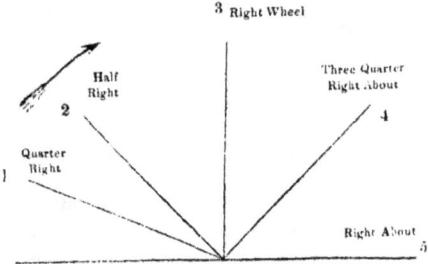

1. Wheeling should at first be practised in single rank, beginning with small Divisions, next increasing to a Troop, and lastly to a Squadron.

2. The different degrees of wheel must be performed at

first from the "Halt," that they may be well understood by the men: afterwards they should be much practised on the move.

3. For attaining good dressing and steadiness, wheeling the whole circle to either hand, with occasional halts, is an excellent practice. When unsteadiness is observed, the men must be halted just as they happen to be at the moment, and the fault pointed out.

4. All wheels of the Squadron and its parts, from the halt, are to be made on a flank; excepting the wheels of Threes, which are made on the centre man of each*.

5. While wheels are in progress, dressing is to the "wheeling" flank, and distance from knee to knee is preserved from the "standing" flank. The pivot man turns his horse on his forefeet, keeps his ground, and comes gradually round with his rank. The outward flank man looks to his rank, regulates the pace at which the wheel is made, and conducts the flank so as to avoid crowding on the rank, the men resisting all pressure from the outward, but giving way to all from the inward flank. All the horses' heads must be kept rather outward, and the croups lightly pressed inwards with the leg. The rear rank must rein back at the standing flank, and partly passage and incline towards the wheeling hand in order to cover.

6. In wheels upon the move, the wheeling flank moves about one-half faster than the rate at which the body is marching.

7. In wheels upon the move, of less than the quarter circle, the pivot only checks and turns his horse during the wheel, and resumes his former pace on the word "*Forward.*"

8. In wheels upon the move, of a degree amounting to the quarter circle or more, the pivot halts and turns his horse during the wheel, and resumes his former pace on the word "*Forward.*"

---

* Unless when Yeomanry Corps are very often assembled, and have a great deal of practice, it is recommended they should always wheel on the flank men of the Threes, as laid down in Sect. IX. for "Threes on the Move."

WHEELING.

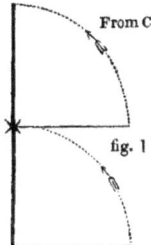

From Column into Line.

fig. 1

9. After wheeling into Line from Column, dressing is to the centre of the Squadron (see fig. 1); and also after the Squadron wheels about, reverses its front, or countermarches in line.

10. After wheeling into echellon, the dressing, at the word "*Forward*," is to the inward hand. (See fig. 2 and 3.)

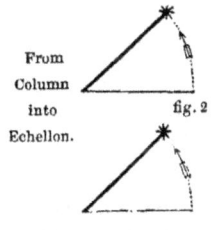

From Column into Echellon. fig. 2

From Line into Echellon. fig. 3

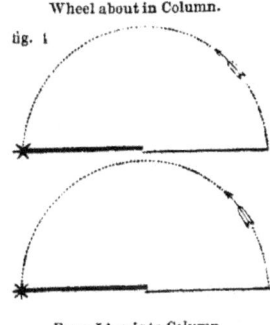

Wheel about in Column.
fig. 4

11. After wheeling about or countermarching Divisions, Troops or Squadrons, in column, the dressing is to whichever flank has become the Pivot. (See fig. 4.)

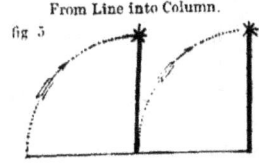

From Line into Column.
fig. 5

12. When there is no "Halt" after wheeling into column, the dressing is to the pivot. (See fig. 5.)

---

* The stars show the flank to which the men dress after the wheels.

13. In the movement of a column of Troops, or Divisions, when a wheel of the quarter circle is to be made in succession, the word "*Forward*" is given, as soon as the wheel is completed.

14. WHEELS ON A MOVEABLE PIVOT. Wheels on a moveable pivot are used in columns of a small front, or when the change of direction to be given is less than the quarter circle.

When wheels or changes of direction of bodies in column are made on a moveable pivot, both flanks are kept in motion; the inner, or flank wheeled to, describing an arc of the lesser circle; the outer or wheeling flank describing an arc of the larger circle; the intermediate men conforming to this movement.

SECTION IX. THREES.

1. WHEELING OF THREES. The wheel is made upon the centre horse of each rank, which must be turned upon his centre, and the right and left of Threes move up, or rein back, according to the hand to which the wheel is made, so as to dress upon the centre man, from whom the distance is taken*.

2. The dressing of Threes, after the wheel, is to the pivot flank; that is, when they wheel to the right, they afterwards dress to the left, and *vice versâ*.

3. When Threes are ordered "*About*," they always wheel to the right about.

4. When the word "*Front*" is given to Threes which have moved to a flank, it implies that such body is to resume its proper front, by wheeling into line again.

5. DISTANCE IN MOVEMENT BY THREES. In the movement by Threes to a flank, the Threes must be as much closed up as is consistent with the free action of the horse. But some extension will unavoidably take place during quick movements, especially in deep and broken ground, therefore the men must

---

* See the note to p. 56.

not be constantly blamed for not closing up, as it only renders the march of the Threes unsteady.

6. WHEEL OF THREES ON THE MOVE. Whenever Threes wheel without halting, each Three is to wheel on its flank man instead of on its centre. When halted in deep ground where the wheel of Threes could not without difficulty be made upon the centre, it may be done in this mode upon the flank; but the Squadron must previously be put in motion.

7. In all movements by Threes the Threes wheel at once, upon the word "*Threes Right*," "*Threes Left*," "*Threes About*," without the word "*March;*" and halt and dress to their Pivots without any word for that purpose. These commands should never be hurried, and a slight pause between the words renders them more distinct.

Section X. PACES.

1. THE rate of Walk from three and a half to four miles an hour.

The Trot to be eight miles and a half an hour as the general pace of manœuvre, but for Squadron Drills and the ordinary exercise of a Regiment, it should be limited to seven miles an hour*.

The Canter to be eleven miles an hour.

2. To practise these paces, a quarter of a mile must be marked out, which the Officers and Non-commissioned Officers will be habituated to pass over, at a Walk, in three minutes and forty-five seconds; at a Trot, in one minute and forty-six seconds, for the rate of eight miles and a half an hour; and, for the slower Trot, in two minutes and nine seconds. The Canter in one minute and twenty-two seconds.

---

* It is recommended to adhere, on all occasions, to seven miles an hour, steadiness being of much more importance to Yeomanry than speed.

PACES.

3. The Canter may be occasionally used for very simple Formations, but it is not to be considered applicable to the general purposes of manœuvre.

4. The rate of Charge should not exceed the speed of the slowest horses*.

5. To preserve that uniformity of movement so essential to order and regularity, the Trot and Canter must commence gradually, and by the whole body at the same time.

Section XI.

FORMATION OF THE TROOP.

1. Each Troop forms on its own parade, in a single rank, according to the size roll, the tallest men and horses being on that flank, which will be the inward one in Squadron. After which the inspection is made as ordered.

2. The Commanding Officer numbers the Troop off from its inward flank, tells off the rear rank, consisting of the smallest men and horses; and forms two deep at close order by filing, or by reining back and passaging†.

3. He places the senior Subaltern in front of the centre, and the junior in the rear.

---

* So much confusion accompanies the charge of Cavalry at all times, even though attended with success, that it is strongly recommended to Yeomanry not to exceed a moderate hand gallop in the practice of attack. The preservation of their steadiness and order by this means would far more than compensate for the decrease of speed upon any serious and critical occasion.

† The rule here given is that of the Regulars; but it is recommended to Yeomanry to form and exercise in single rank, both as a simpler formation, and as more useful and effective on occasions of Riot and Disturbance.

FORMATION OF THE TROOP.

4. He then places a Serjeant on the right and left of the Troop to be Troop Guides; and also two Non-commissioned Officers together, as nearly as he can judge, in the centre of the front rank, who are to become Division Guides.

5. Any remaining Non-commissioned Officers, with the Trumpeter and Farrier, are posted in the rear, at the distance of half a horse's length.

6. If the Troop is to join in Squadron immediately, any further telling off may be dispensed with, until the Squadron is formed, which is done by simply filing to the other Troop, or else being formed upon by it.

7. If the Troop is to act independently, or has any considerable distance to march to the rendezvous of the Squadron, it will be further told off, according to the instructions for the Squadron, in the following section, so far as they are applicable.

Section XII.
FORMATION OF THE SQUADRON.

Squadron in Line.

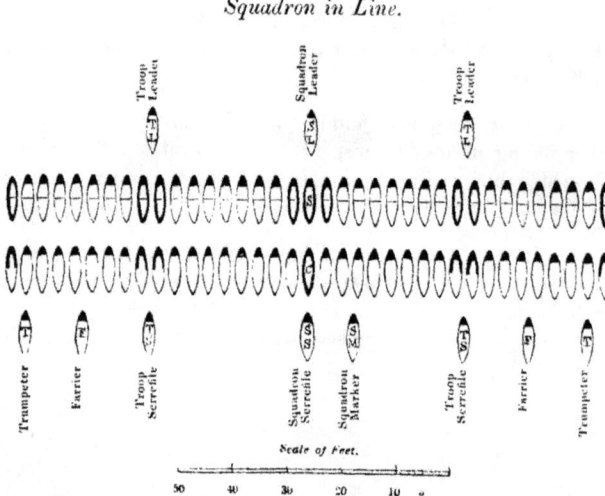

The Standard is represented in this plate as in the centre, the same as in Heavy Cavalry; but it is recommended to have the Standard carried by the right Guide of the left Troop.

1. When the Squadron is to be formed, the two Troops that compose it close in to each other, and the Officers advance two horses' lengths, fronting their Troops*.

---

* When a single Troop of Yeomanry acts in one rank, it should, unless very weak in number, be told off and formed as a Squadron. In this case the whole are cautioned, that they are considered as divided into right Troop and left Troop; intelligent men are named to complete the double number of Officers and Non-commissioned Officers; the Serjeants and acting Serjeants take post as near as they can judge where their places will be: the centre of the intended Squadron is formed by numbering from the right and dividing the whole equally, and the two nearest Serjeants being shifted there, the rest of the posting and telling off proceeds as usual.

FORMATION OF THE SQUADRON. 63

2. The Commanding Officer of the Squadron, having ascertained the number of files in each, equalizes the Troops by shifting a file or two from the inward flank of the stronger Troop, which is done by merely shifting the centre Serjeants of the Squadron the necessary number of files to the right or left[*].

3. The distribution of the Officers is as follows: one in front of the centre of each Troop, (termed the Troop Leaders,) another (who is called the Squadron Serrefile) in rear of the centre of the Squadron, to lead to the rear; one Officer in rear of the centre of each Troop, as Serrefile, at half a horse's length from the rear rank.

4. The Standard is carried by the right Guide of the left Troop.

5. TELLING OFF THE SQUADRON AND POSTING OF NON-COMMISSIONED OFFICERS. The Squadron being thus formed of two Troops, with Non-commissioned Officers, called Troop Guides, and their Coverers on the flanks of each, is ordered to number off from the centre the number of files which it is intended the second and third Divisions should be composed of; the man who last numbered off, and the one next beyond him, hold up their hands to mark the flanks of Divisions, on which the two Non-commissioned Officers, called Division Guides, if not already in those places, move out and post themselves there accordingly, the two or more men passaging right, or left, as may be necessary.

Suppose two Troops to join in Squadron, the right Troop bringing seventeen and the left Troop fifteen files (Guides in the ranks), the Squadron Leader directs the inward flank Guides to move out together to the front, and then orders one file to close from the right to the left Troop: thus equalizing the Troops to sixteen files each; the two Guides then rein back into the vacancy, which is now the centre of the Squadron.

---

[*] In the regular Cavalry, the Troops are equalized by shifting a few files from the outward flank, but as the men do not like quitting their own Troops in the Yeomanry, it is just the same to shift them from the inward flank, so that when the Squadron is in line they are still next their own comrades.

FORMATION OF THE SQUADRON.

He then gives the word "*Tell off Nines from the Centre,*" in accordance with the scale as here laid down. The Centre Serjeants tell *one*, and the men, on each side of them, tell off their numbers up to No. 9 in each Troop. The two Nos. 9 and the men next beyond them extend their hands, and the telling goes no further. The Serjeants, who had placed themselves as near as they could judge two in the centre of each Troop, immediately take the places of the men whose hands are extended, and who make room by closing to whichever side those Serjeants change from, who are thus properly placed as right and left Guides of Divisions.

If the Serjeants happen to have judged their places, so that in numbering it falls to them to extend their hands, they of course do not change at all. If it falls to one of them only (say the nearest to the centre) to extend his hand, they both move out together and shift one place nearer to the centre, the file whom they thus displace passaging to the outside hand of them.

6. The Commanding Officer then orders the men to tell themselves off by Threes and by Files*, beginning at the centre, and telling off to each flank; the File on the right of the Standard telling off "left," and the Standard telling off "right," both by Threes and by Files. The Guides are to be included in these tellings off.

---

* It is recommended to dispense with the telling by files altogether, because it greatly increases the liability of mistake in the important telling by Threes. File-telling is only used at present in the regular Cavalry for dismounting; and an equally good method of dismounting will be found laid down at pp. 95—98.

FORMATION OF THE SQUADRON.

7. The following Scale shows the proportions for Telling off.

Rule for Telling off.	No. in Squadron.	First Division	Second Division	Third Division	Fourth Division
	24	6	6	6	6
	25	6	6	6	7
If the Squadron numbers from 24 to 30 Files, *Tell off Sixes* for the Central Divisions.	26	7	6	6	7
	27	7	6	6	8
	28	8	6	6	8
	29	8	6	6	9
	30	9	6	6	9
	31	6	9	9	7
	32	7	9	9	7
	33	7	9	9	8
	34	8	9	9	8
	35	8	9	9	9
If the Squadron numbers from 31 to 42 Files, *Tell off Nines* for the Central Divisions.	36	9	9	9	9
	37	9	9	9	10
	38	10	9	9	10
	39	10	9	9	11
	40	11	9	9	11
	41	11	9	9	12
	42	12	9	9	12
	43	9	12	12	10
	44	10	12	12	10
	45	10	12	12	11
	46	11	12	12	11
	47	11	12	12	12
If the Squadron numbers from 43 to 54 Files, *Tell off Twelves* for the Central Divisions.	48	12	12	12	12
	49	12	12	12	13
	50	13	12	12	13
	51	13	12	12	14
	52	14	12	12	14
	53	14	12	12	15
Obs.— From 55 to 66, the Central Divisions to be told off *Fifteens*.	54	15	12	12	15

FORMATION OF THE SQUADRON.

8. As soon as the Squadron is told off, the Commanding Officer proves the tellings off by the commands:

"*First and Third Divisions—Proof.*" On which all the men of those Divisions hold out their right hands.

"*As you were.*" They drop them.

"*Flanks of Threes—Proof.*"

"*As you were.*"

The word is then given, "*Officers take Post.*"

9. Posts of Officers and Non-commissioned Officers after the Squadron is formed.

Commanding Officer.	Advanced half a horse's length before the centre.
One Officer.	The same distance in rear of the centre.
Two Officers.	One at the same distance in front of the centre of each Troop.
Two Officers.	One at the same distance in rear of the centre of each Troop.
Troop Serjeant-Major or Serjeant.	Carrying the Standard as Right Guide of the left Troop.
Eight Non-commissioned Officers. (Guides.)	One on each flank of each Division.

One Troop Serjeant-Major as Squadron Marker, at an interval of one horse's length on the right of the Squadron Serrefile; the Trumpeters in rear of the second file from each flank; and all supernumerary Officers and Serjeants, and the Farriers, distributed in one line, at half a horse's length from the rear of the Squadron*.

---

* It is recommended to appoint two or three intelligent men in each Troop to act as Lance Corporals, besides the regular number. They learn to command Divisions, and take more pride in their duty, and yet are equally available as Privates.

FORMATION OF THE SQUADRON.

10. REPLACING OF OFFICERS, &c. In this distribution, if a sufficient number of any rank is not present, Serjeants replace Officers, Corporals replace Serjeants, and Lance Corporals replace Corporals, that the Serrefiles may always be complete*.

11. In order to preserve each Troop entire, it is not material if one Division is a file stronger than another. Farriers are considered as detached, in all situations of manœuvre.

---

* It is a great error to dispense with any of the Serrefiles. Confusion is always more to be feared in retreating than in advancing; and besides the use of them in leading to the rear, they are very necessary for preventing inattention in the ranks.

FORMATION OF THE SQUADRON.

Order.

Squadron at Order.

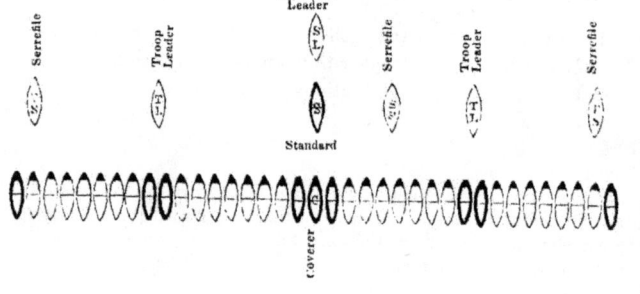

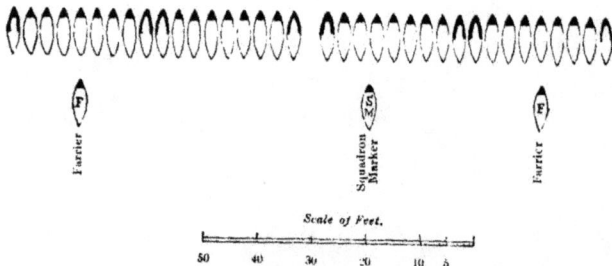

The Standard in this plate is represented the same as in Heavy Cavalry; but it is recommended to have the Standard carried by the right Guide of the left Troop.

12. The Squadron being formed at "Close Order," if "Order" is to be taken, the Commanding Officer gives the word "*Rear Rank take Order*," and the distance of four horses' lengths is immediately marked by the two flank men of the rear rank, who move to the rear, turn about again to the front and dress to the hand ordered. At the word "*March!*" the rear rank reins back, and is dressed upon the flank men.

FORMATION OF THE SQUADRON. 69

13. The Squadron Leader advances two horses' lengths, and the other Officers half a horse's length; the Serrefile Officers move round the flanks and align themselves with them; the senior Subalterns in front of the second file from the outward flanks of their Troops, and the others dividing the ground between the Standard and the Troop Leaders.

14. In Regiments that have Standards, the Right Guide of the left Troop (who should carry the Standard) advances, and aligns himself with the Troop Leaders, his Coverer taking his place. The Squadron Serrefile is between him and the Right Troop Leader.

15. The Trumpeters are on the right of the front rank, at an interval of one horse's length.

16. When from "Order" the Squadron is again to take "Close Order," the caution is given, *"Rear Rank take Close Order;"* and at the word *"March,"* the rear rank moves forward at a trot, to close order, and the Officers and Standard take their posts as before.

Section XIII.

GENERAL RULES ON THE MARCHES AND FORMATIONS BY THREES AND FILES*.

1. The drills must first be practised with squads of from twelve to eighteen men, in single rank; they may then be done by the Troop in two ranks, and finally by the Squadron, with Officers complete.

2. For the practices in these squads, no other telling off is required than that of Threes from the right or left.

3. To avoid repetitions of right and left, the Marches and Formations in the following drill are only laid down with reference to the former hand, but the Marches and Formations must

---

* The whole of these Marches and Formations are as applicable to a formation in single rank as in double: it is only necessary to leave out what regards the rear rank in the instructions.

be executed as often by the left as by the right, and not in regular order, but forming and marching off in different ways, as most convenient.

4. After the men are able to go through the whole correctly at a walk, the Marches and Formations should generally be performed at a trot.

5. In all Marches, care must be taken that the leading Pivot marches upon two points, (as laid down in p. 52,) and that he leads off at a moderate pace.

6. When marching in file, the Instructor occasionally gives the word "*Halt*," and causes the leading file to passage his horse half a yard (say to the right); then cautioning the next man to press his horse to the same hand, so as to cover the leading file's horse, he directs the remainder to take up their covering successively from the front, upon the base thus given by the leading file and the man next behind him. In this manner files or single files may cover in any direction. The same mode of instruction may with advantage be used in covering the pivots of Threes.

7. The drill of a Squad or Troop at two yards' interval from knee to knee, is an excellent practice to create intelligence and good dressing.

8. In executing Formations, the Instructor takes care to place the leading File or Three perfectly square, as they arrive on the intended line, in order that the remainder may have a correct base for their formation; great pains must be taken to prevent any hurry in dressing up, which cannot be done too steadily: it is always better to be behind than before the line.

9. No fault requires so much attention to correct as the hurrying up of the rear during a Formation: the rear must never be suffered to move up the least faster than those who begin the Formation, even although some loss of distances should happen in consequence.

10. The Threes on the flanks should be occasionally changed during the exercise, in order to accustom every man to lead steadily, and acquire readiness in commencing all Marches and Formations.

Substitution for SECTION XIV.

MARCHES TO THE FLANKS, FRONT, AND REAR, BY THREES AND FILES.

Marches to the Right.

BY THREES.

"*Threes Right*." The whole wheel "Threes right." (fig. 1.)

"*March*." The whole move off together. (fig. 2.)

BY SECTIONS OF THREES.

"*Sections of Threes to the Right*." "*Threes Right*," the whole wheel "Threes right." (fig. 3.)

"*March*." The leading Three of the front rank marches straight forward, its rear rank inclining and covering it: the remainder move off their ground in succession in the same manner; first a front-rank Three, and then a rear-rank Three, alternately. (fig. 4.)

BY FILES.

"*Files Right*." "*March*." The right-hand men of both ranks turn to the right, (the rear-rank man closing to his front-rank man,) and march straight forward: the remainder move off their ground in succession, front and rear-rank men together, as it comes to their turn. (fig. 5.)

BY SINGLE FILES.

"*Single Files Right*." "*March*." The right-hand man of the front rank turns to the right, and marches straight forward, followed by his rear-rank man; the remainder move off their ground in succession in the same manner; first a front-rank man and then a rear-rank man, alternately. (fig. 6.)

Marches from the Right to the Front.

By Threes.

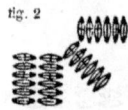

fig. 1

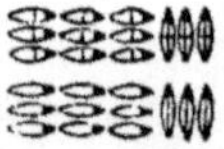

"*Advance by Threes from the Right.*" "*Threes Right.*" The right-hand Three both of the front and rear rank stands fast; the remainder wheel Threes right. (fig. 1.)

fig. 2

"*March.*" The right-hand Three of the front rank moves straight to the front; its rear-rank Three moves up to it by inclining; the remainder move on and wheel to the left at the same point from which the right-hand Three advanced. (fig. 2)

By Sections of Threes.

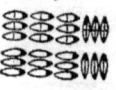

fig. 3

"*Advance by Sections of Threes from the Right.*" "*Threes Right.*" The right-hand Three both of the front and rear rank stands fast; the remainder wheel "Threes Right." (fig. 3.)

fig. 4

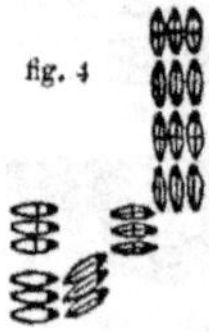

"*March.*" The leading Three marches straight to the front, followed by its rear rank; the remainder move off their ground in succession; first a front-rank and then a rear-rank Three, alternately, and wheel to the left at the same point from which the leading Three advanced. (fig. 4.)

By Files.

fig. 5

"*Advance by Files from the Right.*" "*March.*" The right-hand man of the front rank marches straight to the front, his rear-rank man moving up on his right; the remainder move off their ground in succession, front and rear-rank men together, as it comes to their turn, wheeling to the left when they arrive at the point from which the leading File advanced. (fig. 5.)

By Single Files.

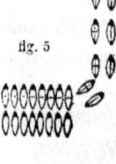

fig. 6

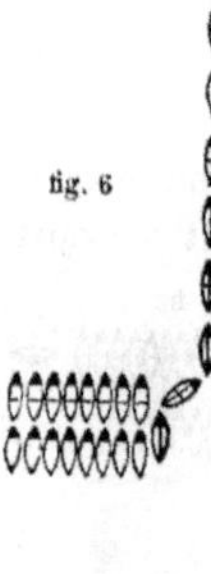

"*Advance by Single Files from the Right.*" "*March.*" The right-hand man of the front rank marches straight to the front, followed by his rear-rank man; the remainder move off their ground in succession; first a front-rank, and then a rear-rank man, alternately, and wheel to the left at the same point from which the leading man advanced. (fig. 6.)

Marches from the Right to the Rear.

By Threes.

"*Retire by Threes from the Right.*" "*Threes Right,*" the whole wheel "Threes Right." (fig. 1.) "*March,*" followed by "*Right Wheel;*" the leading Threes, wheeling to the right, receive the word "*Forward,*" and march straight to the rear, the remainder following and wheeling to the right at the same point from which the leading Threes retired. (fig. 2.)

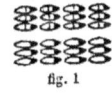
fig. 1

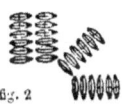
fig. 2

By Sections of Threes.

"*Retire by Sections of Threes from the Right.*" "*Threes Right,*" the whole wheel "Threes Right," (fig. 3.) "*March,*" followed by *Right Wheel;* the leading front-rank Three, advancing one yard and wheeling again to the right, marches straight to the rear, followed by its rear-rank Three; the remainder move off their ground in succession, first a front-rank, and then a rear-rank Three, alternately, each wheeling to the right at the same point from which the leading Threes retired. (fig. 4.)

fig. 3

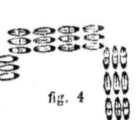
fig. 4

By Files.

"*Retire by Files from the Right.*" "*March.*" The right-hand men of both ranks turn to the right-about, and the rear-rank man waiting till his front-rank man moves up on his left, they both march straight to the rear; the remainder move off their ground in succession, front and rear-rank men together, as it comes to their turn, wheeling to their right when they arrive at the same point from which the leading File retired. (fig. 5.)

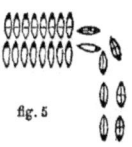
fig. 5

By Single Files.

"*Retire by Single Files from the Right.*" "*March.*" The right-hand man of the front rank turns about and marches straight to the rear, followed by his rear-rank man; the remainder move off their ground in succession; first a front-rank and then a rear-rank man, alternately, each turning to his right as he arrives at the same point from which the leading man retired. (fig. 6.)

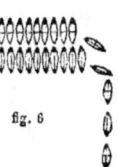
fig. 6

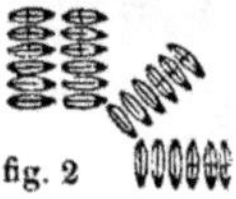

"*March.*" The leading Threes, wheeling to the right, receive the word "*Forward*," and march straight to the rear, the remainder following and wheeling to the right at the same point from which the leading Threes retired (fig. 2).

fig. 2

By Sections of Threes.

fig. 3

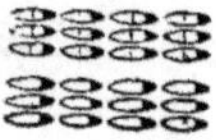

"*Retire by Sections of Threes from the Right.*" The whole wheel "Threes right" (fig. 3).

"*March.*" The leading Threes wheel again to the right, the same as above, and the leading Three of the front rank marches straight to the rear, followed by its rear-rank Three, which checks its pace, inclines, and covers it; the remainder move off their ground in succession, first a front-rank, and then a rear-rank Three, alternately, each wheeling to the right at the same point from which the leading Threes retired (fig. 4).

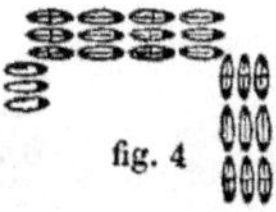

fig. 4

By Files.

"*Retire by Files from the Right.*" The right-hand men of both ranks turn to the right-about, and the front-rank man moves up on the left of his rear-rank man: the remainder turn their horses' heads to the right (fig. 5).

fig. 5

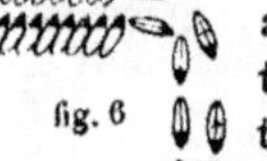

"*March.*" The leading File marches straight to the rear; the remainder move off their ground in succession, front and rear-rank men together, as it comes to their turn, wheeling to their right when they arrive at the same point from which the leading File retired (fig. 6).

fig. 6

TO THE REAR.

By Single Files.

"*Retire by Single Files from the Right.*" The right-hand men of both ranks turn to the right-about, and the front-rank man moves upon the left of his rear-rank man; the remainder turn their horses' heads to the right (fig. 7).

"*March.*" The leading man of the front rank marches straight to the rear, followed by his rear-rank man; the remainder move off their ground in succession; first a front-rank and then a rear-rank man, alternately, each turning to his right as he arrives at the same point from which the leading man retired (fig. 8).

Section XV.

FORMATIONS TO THE FRONT, FLANKS, AND REAR, FROM THREES AND FILES.

Formations to the Front*.

From Threes.

"*Front Form.*" The leading Three of the front rank continues to advance for three horses' lengths, and then halts, its rear-rank Three, checking its pace, moving by an incline to its proper distance, and covering it; the rest of the rear-rank Threes check their pace till the front-rank Threes of the rank next behind come up abreast of them, the whole moving up into line with the leading Threes by inclining to the left (fig. 1).

---

* It must be recollected that all the Formations from Threes and Files are to be performed on the move without any preparatory halt. It is only for the first explanations that the leading Three or File may be moved up separately and placed on its ground.

FORMATIONS TO THE FRONT.

From Sections of Threes.

fig. 2

"*Front Form.*" The leading Three of the front rank continues to advance for three horses' lengths and then halts, its rear-rank Three moving up to its proper distance and covering it, and the remainder moving up into line by inclining to the left (fig. 2).

fig. 3

From Files.

"*Front Form.*" The leading man of the front rank continues to advance for three horses' lengths, and then halts, his rear-rank man moving up to his proper distance, and covering him; the rest of the rear-rank men check their pace, till the front-rank men of the File next behind come up abreast of them; the whole moving up into line with the leading File by inclining to the left (fig. 3).

fig. 4

From Single File.

"*Front Form.*" The leading man of the front rank continues to advance for three horses' lengths, and then halts, his rear-rank man moving up to his proper distance, and covering him; the remainder moving up into line by inclining to the left (fig. 4).

OBSERVATIONS. In Formations to the front, immediately on issuing from narrow ways or streets, it is impossible for the rear, who are not yet clear of the defile, to incline at once towards their places in line; on these occasions, therefore, the Formation of all but the head of the Column becomes the same as laid down for "Formations to the Reverse Flank," since all, excepting the leading men, turn to the left as they come out of the defile, and march along the rear of those already formed, till they come opposite the places where they are to move up into line.

Formations to the Left.

From Threes.

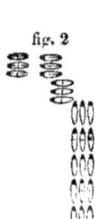

fig. 1

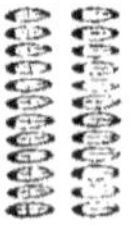

"*Halt Front.*" N.B. In this case the word "*Front*" is employed instead of "*Left Form.*"

The whole of the Threes wheel to the left, and close to whichever hand is the point of dressing (fig. 1).

From Sections of Threes.

fig. 2

"*Left Form.*" The leading Three wheels to the left, and moves up three horses' lengths, followed by its rear rank; the remainder continue moving on, and as each Three arrives opposite its place, it wheels to the left, and forms up to the rank to which it belongs (fig. 2).

From Files.

fig. 3

"*Left Form.*" The leading File wheels to the left, and the front-rank man advancing three horses' lengths, his rear-rank man follows him; the remainder continue moving on, and as each File arrives opposite its place, it wheels to the left, and each man forms up to the rank to which he belongs (fig. 3).

From Single Files.

fig. 4

"*Left Form.*" The leading man turns to the left, and moves up three horses' lengths, followed by his rear-rank man; the remainder continue moving on, and as each man arrives opposite his place he turns to the left, and forms up to the rank to which he belongs (fig. 4).

Formations to the Reverse Flank.

From Threes.

"*To the Reverse Flank*," "*Right Form.*" The rear-rank Threes check their pace till the front-rank Threes of the rank next behind come up abreast of them; in the mean time, the leading Three of the front rank wheels to the right, and advances

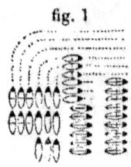

three horses' lengths beyond the right flank of the Column, and halts; its rear-rank wheeling to the right, covering it, and moving up to the proper distance; the remainder continue moving on, each Three wheeling to the right when opposite its place, and forming up to the rank to which it belongs (fig. 1).

From Sections of Threes.

"*To the Reverse Flank*," "*Right Form.*" The leading Three of the front rank wheels to the right, advances three horses'

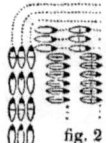

lengths, and halts; its rear-rank Three arriving behind it, wheels, covers, and moves up to its proper distance; the remainder continue moving on, and as each Three arrives opposite its place it wheels to the right, and forms up to the rank to which it belongs (fig. 2).

From Files.

"*To the Reverse Flank*," "*Right Form.*" The rear-rank man of each File checks his pace till the front-rank man of the File next behind comes up abreast of him; in the mean time, the leading man of the front rank turns to the right, advances three

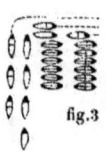

horses' lengths beyond the right flank of the Column, and halts; his rear-rank man wheeling to the right, covering him, and moving up to his proper distance; the remainder continue moving on, each man turning to the right when opposite his place, and forming up to the rank to which he belongs (fig. 3).

FORMATIONS TO THE REVERSE FLANK.   79

From Single Files.

"*To the Reverse Flank*," "*Right Form.*" The leading man of the front rank turns to the right, advances three horses' lengths, and halts; his rear-rank man arriving behind him, turns, covers, and moves up to his proper distance; the remainder continue moving on, and as each man arrives opposite his place he turns to the right, and forms up to the rank to which he belongs (fig. 4).

Formations to the Right about.

From Threes.

"*Right about Form.*" The rear-rank Threes check their pace till the front-rank Threes next behind come up abreast of them; in the mean time the leading Three of the front rank wheels to its right, advances enough to clear the flank of the Column by half a horse's length, wheels again to its right, advances three horses' lengths, and halts; its rear rank makes two wheels to the right, follows and covers at the proper distance; the remainder continue moving on, wheeling to the right at the same point, passing along the rear of those already formed, and forming up to the ranks to which they belong, as they come opposite their places (fig. 1).

From Sections of Threes.

"*Right about Form.*" The leading Three of the front rank wheels to the right, advances enough to clear the flank of the Column by half a horse's length, wheels again to its right, advances three horses' lengths, and halts; its rear rank makes two wheels to the right, in like manner, when it has reached the same point, following and covering at the proper distance; the remainder continue moving on, wheeling to the right at the same point, passing along the rear of those already formed, and forming up to the ranks to which they belong when they come opposite their places (fig. 2).

FORMATIONS TO THE RIGHT-ABOUT.

From Files.

"*Right about Form.*" The rear-rank men check their pace till the front-rank man of the File next behind comes up abreast of each; in the mean time the leading man of the front rank wheels to the right, advances enough to clear the flank of the Column by half a horse's length, wheels again to the right, advances three horses' lengths, and halts; the remainder continue moving on, wheeling to the right at the same point, passing along the rear of those already formed, and forming up to the ranks to which they belong as they come opposite their places (fig. 3).

From Single Files.

"*Right about Form.*" The leading man turns to the right, advances half a horse's length, turns again to the right, advances three horses' lengths, and halts; his rear-rank man makes two wheels in like manner, as he arrives at the same point, following and covering at the proper distance; the remainder continue moving on, wheeling to the right at the same point, passing along the rear of those already formed, and forming up to the ranks to which they belong as they come opposite their places (fig. 4).

Section XVI.

COUNTERMARCH, AND REVERSING THE FRONT, OF THE SQUADRON.

Countermarch.

The effect of a Countermarch is, that the front and rear rank change places, and the Line fronts the contrary way to what it did before.

The Squadron in Line (fig. 1) receives the caution.

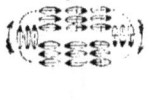

fig. 1

"*The Squadron will Countermarch,*" followed by "*Threes Right and Left,*" on which the front rank wheel "Threes right;" and the rear rank wheel "Threes left" (fig. 2)*.

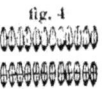

fig. 2

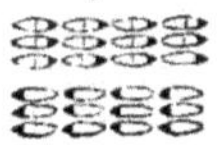

On the word "*March,*" the leading Three of each rank advances half a horse's length, and wheels to the right-about on its right-hand man, and the whole follow, and wheel at the same point, until the front and rear rank have changed places (fig. 3); immediately upon which the word "*Halt, Front, Dress,*" is given (fig. 4).

fig. 3

fig. 4

Observation. Whenever a Squadron, Troop, or Division countermarches, the Front rank invariably wheel "Threes right," and the Rear rank "Threes left," without reference to which flank may be the Pivot.

Reversing the Front.

The Squadron should be frequently practised to "Reverse its Front," in the following manner:

"*Reverse the Front by the wheel about of Troops—Right Troop Advance—March.*" The Right Troop advances a distance

---

* When there is no rear rank, the front rank moves just the same as if there were one.

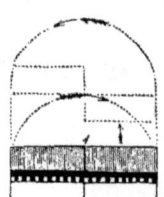

equal to its front, and as soon as the Leader of the Left Troop judges he shall have room, he gives the word, *Right about wheel—March*," followed by "*Halt, Dress*," at the completion of the wheel. His word to "wheel" is the signal for the Leader of the Right Troop to give that Troop the word "*Left about wheel*," followed by "*Forward*" at the completion of the wheel, and "*Halt, Dress up*," when on a line with the rear rank of the Left Troop. It must in this exercise be an invariable rule for the Right Troop to be that which advances.

Section XVII.

DIMINUTION AND INCREASE OF FRONT.

Diminishing the Front from the Halt.

1. FROM SQUADRON TO TROOPS. When the Squadron is to diminish its front to Troops, the caution is given, "*Advance by Troops from the Right*," on which the Leader of the Right Troop, taking his post in front of the second File from the left, gives the word "*Right Troop Advance*." On the word "*March*" that Troop advances, and, just before his right flank is cleared by it, the Leader of the Left Troop, taking post in like manner, gives the word "*Left Troop—Right incline—March*," followed by "*Forward*" as soon as it covers in Column.

2. FROM TROOPS TO DIVISIONS. When the Squadron, standing in Open Column of Troops, is to diminish its front to Divisions, the caution is given "*Advance by Divisions from the Right*," on which the Leader of the Right Troop gives the word "*First Division Advance*." On the word "*March*," that Division advances, and just before the flank of the second is cleared by it, he adds, "*Second Division—Right incline—March;*" the left

DIMINISHING THE FRONT. 83

Guide of that Division giving the word "*Forward*," as soon as it covers the first Division. The Troop Leader then takes his proper place in Column (see p. 108, Art. 9). At the same time the Left Troop forms Divisions in the same way. So that the first and third Divisions advance, and the second and fourth incline, at the same moment.

3. If the Squadron is at once to march off to its front in Column of Divisions, the caution is given, "*Advance by Divisions from the Right.*" The Squadron Leader gives the words "*First Division Advance*"—"*Remaining Divisions Right Wheel.*" On the word "*March,*" the first Division moves straight forward, and the others wheel and receive from their Squadron Leader the word "*Forward*"—then, in succession, at the proper point, "*Left Wheel,*" from their respective Troop Leaders and Division Guides, and "*Forward.*"

4. FROM DIVISIONS TO THREES. When the Squadron, standing in Open Column of Divisions, is to diminish its front to Threes, the caution is given, "*Advance by Threes from the Right;*" and on the word "*March,*" each Division advances in Column of Threes from its right, as laid down for the "March from Right to Front" (p. 72, SECT. XIV.) By this means all the Divisions fall into one Column of Threes.

5. FROM THREES TO SECTIONS OF THREES. When the Squadron, standing in Column of Threes, is to diminish its front to Sections of Threes, the caution is given "*Advance by Sections of Threes,*" repeated by the Leader of the Right Troop; and on the word "*March,*" the leading Three of the front rank advances straight; its rear-rank Three inclines to the left until it covers, and follows; the remainder move off in succession in the same manner, first a front-rank Three and then a rear-rank Three alternately. The other Troop moves off in due time, by the same word from its Leader, and in the same way.

6. FROM SECTIONS OF THREES TO FILES. When the Squadron, standing in Column of Sections of Threes, is to diminish its front to Files, the caution is given, "*Advance by Files,*" repeated by the Leader of the Right Troop. On the word "*March,*" the right-hand man of the leading Three advances straight,

followed by his Centre and Left, their rear-rank men filing from the right, and trotting up abreast of them. The remainder move off in the same way, as it comes to their turn; the other Troop moves off in due time, by the same word from its Leader, and in the same way.

7. FROM FILES TO SINGLE FILES. When the Squadron standing in File, is to diminish its front to Single Files, the caution is given, "*Advance by Single Files,*" repeated by the Leader of the Right Troop. On the word "*March,*" the leading man of the front rank advances straight; his rear-rank man inclines to the left, covers, and follows; the remainder move off their ground as it comes to their turn; first a front-rank man, and then a rear-rank man, alternately. The other Troop follows in due time, by the same word from its Leader, and in the same way.

8. FROM THREES TO FILES. The Squadron breaks at once from "Threes" to Files, by the word "*Advance by Files,*" repeated by the Leader of the Right Troop. On the word "*March,*" the right-hand men of the leading Threes advance, followed by their Centres and Lefts, the rear rank closing to their front rank. The other Troop follows in due time, by the same word from its Leader, and in the same way.

9. FROM THREES TO SINGLE FILE. To diminish at once from Threes to Single File, the caution is given, "*Advance by Single Files,*" repeated by the Leader of the Right Troop. On the word "*March,*" the right-hand man of the leading front-rank Section moves off, followed by his rear-rank man, who inclines to the left, covers, and follows him; the remainder move off in the same manner, front and rear-rank men alternately, as it comes to their turn. The other Troop follows in due time, by the same word from its Leader, and in the same way.

Diminishing the Front on the Move.

1. FROM SQUADRON TO TROOPS. When the Squadron, on the march, is to diminish its Front to Troops, the caution is given, "*Form Troops,*" on which the Leader of the Left Troop gives the words "*Left Troop Halt—Right incline—March,*" and

then taking post in front of the second File from the left "*Forward*," as soon as it covers in Column.

2. FROM TROOPS TO DIVISIONS. When the Squadron marching in Column of Troops, is to diminish its front to Divisions, the caution is given, "*Form Divisions*," on which the Leader of the Right Troop gives the words, "*Second Division, Halt—Right incline—March;*" and then takes his proper place in Column (see p. 108, Art. 9): the left Guide of the second Division gives the word "*Forward*," when it has gained its covering. The Leader of the Left Troop doubles back the fourth Division at the same moment and in the same way.

3. FROM DIVISIONS TO THREES. The Squadron marching in Column of Divisions, and arriving at a place where the front must be diminished to Threes, the caution is given, "*Advance by Threes from the Right;*" and each Division moves off from its right, on the principle prescribed in SECT. XIV., for the "March from Right to Front."

OBSERVATIONS. In diminishing from Threes to Sections; from Sections to Files; from Files to Single File; and from Threes to File; the whole must first be halted for an instant, and the operation then proceeds as laid down for Diminishing the Front from the Halt. Should there be more Squadrons than one to pass the obstacle, each Squadron will be put in motion in sufficient time for its head to arrive at the obstacle close after the rear of that which last diminished its front; it will then be halted for an instant only, and proceed in like manner, that no distance may be lost.

Increasing the Front from the Halt.

1. FROM SINGLE FILE TO FILES. The Squadron standing in Single File, the caution is given, "*Form Files*," repeated by Troop Leaders; the leading front-rank man advances three horses' lengths, and his rear-rank man forms upon his right. On the word "*March*," the remainder move off at a walk, each File forming when it arrives at the File which formed last.

2. FROM FILES TO SECTIONS OF THREES. The Squadron standing in File, the caution is given, "*Form Sections of Threes*,"

repeated by Troop Leaders; the leading front-rank man advances three horses' lengths, his rear-rank man inclines to the left and covers him. ~~On the word~~ "*March*," their Centres and Lefts move up abreast of them, the remainder following, and each Section of Threes forming when it arrives at those which formed last.

3. FROM SECTIONS OF THREES TO THREES. The Squadron standing in Sections of Threes, the caution is given, "*Form Threes*," repeated by Troop Leaders; the leading front-rank Three advances three horses' lengths, the leading rear-rank Three inclines to the right and dresses up to it. On the word "*March*," the remainder move off at a walk, each Three forming when it arrives at those which formed last.

4. FROM THREES TO DIVISIONS. The Squadron standing in Threes, the caution is given, "*Form Divisions*," repeated by Troop Leaders. On the word "*March*," the leading front-rank section of each Division advances three horses' lengths and halts; the remainder of each Division inclining and forming on their own leading sections in the manner laid down for the Formation to the Front from Threes, in SECT. XV.*, p. 75.

5. FROM DIVISIONS TO TROOPS. The Squadron standing in Column of Divisions, the caution is given, "*Form Troops*." The Leader of the Right Troop gives the word "*First Division Advance—Second Division Left incline;*" and the Leader of the Left Troop, "*Third Division Advance—Fourth Division Left incline.*" On the word "*March*," the first and third Divisions advance three horses' lengths, and receive from their Troop Leaders the word "*Halt Dress.*" The second and fourth Divisions incline to the left, and receive from their right Guides the word "*Forward*," when the right flank is uncovered; and "*Halt, Dress up*," when their Front rank is in line with the Rear rank of the Divisions formed on. The Troop Leaders place themselves where their left flank will arrive, in order to see that these Divisions dress to the Pivot as soon as formed, and then take their proper place in front of the second Files.

---

* If a rear rank is used, the last rear-rank section of each Division, except the rear one, is prevented inclining by the leading section of the next Division, it must therefore advance straight till it gets room.

INCREASING THE FRONT. 87

6. From Troops to Squadron. The Squadron standing in Column of Troops, the caution is given, "*Form Squadron,*" on which the Leader of the Right Troop gives the word "*Right Troop Advance,*" and the Leader of the Left Troop "*Left Troop, Left incline.*" On the word "*March,*" the Right Troop advancing three horses' lengths, its Leader gives the word "*Halt, Dress,*" and takes post in front of its centre; the Left Troop at the same time inclines to the left until its right flank is uncovered, when its Leader gives the word "*Forward,*" followed by "*Halt, Dress up,*" when its front rank is in line with the rear rank of the other Troop, and then takes post in front of the centre of his Troop.

Increasing the Front on the Move.

1. From Single File to Files. The Squadron arriving in Single File at the spot where the front is to be increased to Files, receives the word "*Form Files,*" repeated by the Troop Leaders, who add the word "*Trot.*" The leading front-rank man continues to walk steadily forward; his rear-rank man trots up on his right, and takes up the walk. The remainder move on at a trot, each File forming as it arrives at those which last formed, and then dropping into the walk.

2. From Files to Sections of Threes. The Squadron arriving in Files at the spot where the front is to be increased to Sections of Threes, receives the word "*Form Sections of Threes,*" repeated by Troop Leaders, who add the word "*Trot.*" The leading front-rank man walks steadily forward, and his centre and left trot up upon his left. The leading rear-rank man checks his pace, inclines and covers his front rank, while his Centre and Left trot into their places on his left. The remainder move on at a trot, each Three forming as it arrives at those which formed last, and then dropping into the walk.

3. From Sections of Threes to Threes. The Squadron arriving in Sections of Threes at the spot where the front is to be increased to Threes, receives the word "*Form Threes,*" repeated by Troop Leaders, who also add the word "*Trot.*" The leading Three continues to walk steadily forward; its rear-rank Three

inclines to the right, and trots up abreast of it. The remainder move on at a trot, each Three forming when they arrive at those which formed last, and then dropping into the walk.

4. FROM FILES TO THREES. The Squadron forms at once from Files to Threes by the word "*Form Threes*," repeated by Troop Leaders, who add the word "*Trot*," on which the leading Three of the front rank form as before directed; the "Right" of Threes of the rear rank inclines a yard to the right, the "Centre" moves straight forward, the "Left" inclines a yard to the left, and both form up to the "Right" of Threes, and dress by the front rank. The remainder move up in File, and form in the same manner.

5. FROM THREES TO DIVISIONS. The Squadron arriving in Threes at the spot where the front is to be increased to Divisions, receives the word "*Form Divisions*," repeated by Troop Leaders, who also add the word "*Trot*." Each Division forms to the front, as laid down (p. 75) for the "Formation from Threes," and then drops into the walk*.

6. FROM DIVISIONS TO TROOPS. The Squadron arriving in Column of Divisions at the spot where the front is to be increased to Troops, receives the word "*Form Troops*," on which the Right Troop Leader gives the word "*Second Division, Left incline, Trot*," and the Left Troop Leader gives his word in like manner to the fourth Division. As these Divisions come up with the first and third, which continue to walk steadily forward, their right Guides give the words "*Forward*," and "*Walk*," when in line with the Divisions formed on. Troop Leaders place themselves where their left flanks will arrive, to see that the men dress to the Pivot, and then take their proper places in front of the second Files.

7. FROM TROOPS TO SQUADRON. The Squadron arriving in Column of Troops at the spot where it is intended to form Squadron, receives the caution "*Form Squadron*," on which the

---

* As the last rear-rank section of each Division is prevented inclining by the leading section of the next Division, it must advance straight till it gets room.

INCREASING THE FRONT.

Left Troop Leader gives the word "*Left Troop, Left incline, Trot.*" As soon as his right flank is uncovered, he gives the word "*Forward*," followed by "*Walk*," on arriving in line with the Right Troop, which meantime continues walking steadily forward. The moment the Squadron is thus formed, Troop Leaders take post in front of the centre of their Troops.

8. FROM DIVISIONS TO SQUADRON. The Squadron moving in Column of Divisions may form at once to the front by word from the Squadron Leader, "*Form Squadron.*" "*Rear Divisions, Left incline, Trot;*" on which they proceed as directed in the preceding paragraph. When the Squadron is formed, its Leader gives the word "*Eyes Centre;*" (or "*Eyes Left,*" if the Squadron is supposed part of a Regimental Column, right in front.)

OBSERVATIONS. When the "Increasing" of Front is performed by the Squadron marching at a trot, the Troop Leaders give the word "*Gallop*" instead of "*Trot*," and "*Trot*" instead of "*Walk*," but this rate must not be attempted till complete steadiness has been attained. Great care must be taken in all these exercises that the rear do not move up in the least degree faster than the regular pace ordered.

SECTION XVIII.

ADVANCE OF THE SQUADRON.

1. MARCH IN LINE. The Squadron being halted and dressed, the "Leader" must take care that he is exactly placed before the Standard, or, (where there is no Standard,) before the Right Guide of the left Troop, and square with respect to the front of the Squadron.

2. LINE OF MARCH TAKEN. In the Advance he will direct his march upon two objects; and as it is not always easy to find them in the distance, such as trees, houses, &c., all Officers should acquire the habit of readily selecting marks upon the ground, at no great distance, such as small stones, or tufts of grass, and so taking fresh ones in the same line, as they advance upon those first selected (see SECT. V., p. 53).

The Leader gives the caution "*The Squadron will advance*," and at the word "*March*," each man puts his horse in motion, and dresses towards the Centre by a glance of the eyes, but without at all turning his head.

3. ATTENTION OF SQUADRON LEADERS. It is the great business of a Leader of a Squadron to carry it forward in its exact perpendicular direction, and he must avoid looking back too often to give orders.

4. ATTENTION OF TROOP OFFICERS AND SERREFILES. The Troop Leaders will take care to align themselves exactly with the Squadron Leader, and preserve the regulated distance from him; and it is the duty of the Serrefiles to watch over the movements of the rear rank, as well as the opening out or closing in of the front.

5. ATTENTION OF THE STANDARD-BEARER, OR RIGHT GUIDE OF THE LEFT TROOP. It must be his object to keep half a horse's length from the Leader; to follow him exactly; and to slacken or quicken his pace, according to the words of command or directions he receives; but any alteration of his pace must be very gradual, because hurrying or springing forward would occasion a shake throughout the Squadron.

6. ATTENTION OF THE RANKS. The attention of the rest of the Squadron should be invariably fixed towards the Centre; but each man and horse must be perfectly square to the front, the dressing being preserved by a glance of the eye, and never by turning the head. The flanks of the Squadron are to be kept rather back, and never on any account before the centre.

The distance of Files is taken and preserved from the Centre of the Squadron. This is more immediately the business of the front rank. The rear rank, at the same time that they dress to their Centre, cover their File Leaders.

7. ALTERATION OF DIRECTION. If an alteration is to be made in the direction of the Squadron, the Leader gradually circles into such new direction, to which the Squadron conforms by advancing one flank and retaining the other till the change is effected. But the defects of an Advance in line must be very gradually corrected.

ADVANCE OF THE SQUADRON.

When the ground is sufficiently extensive, the Squadron should make long advances, changing the pace often, but attentively preserving the due rate of each pace. The Squadron, during its Advance, should be as often accustomed to diminish the paces as to increase them.

8. FILING OVER BROKEN GROUND. While the Squadron is advancing in line, it should sometimes be practised in breaking off from the right of Threes for the purpose of passing over rough or broken ground. The word will be given, "*Single Files from the Right of Threes,*" upon which the "Right" of each front-rank Section continues moving on, followed by his rear-rank man, the "Centres" and "Lefts" of both ranks checking their pace, inclining to their right, and falling into file as they get room. The "Rights" of Threes must carefully preserve the dressing, as well as the intervals which are made by the "Centres" and "Lefts" dropping back. The Squadron again forms Line by the word "*Front form Ranks.*"

9. HALT OF THE SQUADRON. At the word "*Halt*." both Officers and Men remain steady. If ordered to dress they correct their dressing to the proper point. When one Movement is immediately to succeed another, a critical dressing should not be required.

SECTION XIX.

PREPARATION OF THE SQUADRON FOR REGIMENTAL MOVEMENT*.

1. ALTHOUGH the exercise of a single Squadron does not give opportunities for attaining a perfect knowledge of the Movements of a Regiment in the field, it will, nevertheless, afford the means of thoroughly instructing both Officers and Men in Passaging, Reining back, Wheeling, Counter-marching, Advancing, Inclining, Increasing and Decreasing the Front, and also in most of the Movements laid down for the practice of the Regiment.

---

* A single Troop of Yeomanry should always form and exercise as a Squadron, the Officers' places being filled by Non-commissioned Officers, if there are not enough Officers present, and Lance Corporals and well-trained men acting as Guides, where required.

PREPARATION FOR REGIMENTAL MOVEMENT.

2. In the progress of instruction much may be taught by the use of a Skeleton Squadron acting on the flank of a complete one. The Skeleton Squadron will be composed of Guides with their Coverers representing the flanks of Divisions, who must take the utmost care to preserve the same extent of front which their Divisions may be supposed to occupy. When there is a want of Officers, their places must on no account be left vacant, but must be filled by Non-commissioned Officers, and an opportunity will thus be afforded of practising and instructing any number of Non-commissioned Officers. When the Squadron is weak, this exercise may be practised in Single Rank.

The Formations should be made alternately upon either Squadron, the regular words of command being given in the same manner as for a Regiment of two Squadrons.

3. Both Squadron and Troop Leaders must be taught to glance their eyes occasionally to both flanks of the bodies they command, that they may notice any inattention in the ranks. Serrefiles must allow no carelessness of the rear rank to pass unobserved.

4. Upon the Caution being given for a Movement, the Base should be instantly placed. Each Squadron Marker should have a thorough knowledge of the direction in which he is to look for the point he is to dress upon; and in taking his post, he should turn his horse in such a manner as to keep the Base always in view.

5. The Squadron should be often practised in attacking to the Front according to the principles laid down in SECT. IX., PART III., p. 122, and retiring immediately from one or both Flanks by Threes; or in Column of Divisions if strong enough, or by "*Troops outwards about Wheel.*"

6. Some degree of confusion is almost inevitable after a Charge, and to show the means by which order is restored, the Squadron should occasionally be directed to disperse after a Charge, and again rally to the Front, Rear, or Flank, at a Trumpet Signal, but this is an exercise to be used with discretion, for fear of leading to unsteadiness.

7. The practice of Dismounting to act on foot, of Skirmishing, and Outpost duty, must also be attended to.

Section XX.

INSTRUCTION OF OFFICERS.

1. GREAT pains must be taken in the instruction of Officers in every detail of their executive duty in the field. The Troop Leaders must especially be trained to the utmost correctness of movement in their own persons. It is not always sufficient for the Instructor to tell a young Officer what he is to do; but he should place one of his Assistants in command of the Troop for the moment, and cause him to show the right method of executing it.

2. For the purpose of instructing Officers to move small bodies with facility into a new Position, a Base is to be placed at a certain distance from the Squadron, to represent the new Alignment, in front, on either flank, or in the rear. The Officer is then to be directed to lead the Squadron into this Alignment, by entering it either at a front or rear point, and then forming line. For variety of practice, the new position should be marked at various angles with the old one. The Squadron may move in column, either of Troops, Divisions, or Threes, for this practice.

Every Officer should be taught to take up points of Formation, as laid down in SECT. VI., PART III., p. 117, as nothing so well illustrates the general principles of Alignments.

Section XXI. LINKING HORSES.

It may sometimes be convenient to link the horses, to enable the men to parade on foot, or for other purposes.

1. The word is then given "*To link Horses—Prepare to Dismount,*" on which each man unfastens his collar rein or chain, and the dismounting proceeds as usual. When all are dismounted, the word is given "*Rights and Lefts of Threes, Dress up to your Centres;*" on which they move their horses into line with the Centres, the latter stepping a short pace to the right, close to their horses' shoulders. At the word "*Link Horses,*" each man steps out a pace with the right foot, faces about, fronts his horse's head, and links, or fastens his horse with the chain or rein, under the bridle reins, to the collar ring of the horse next to him; it being observed as a rule, that the horses are always to be linked towards the centre of the Squadron or Troop. The collar rein or chain is to be unfastened on the caution.

2. If the men should be called away upon any duty, a sufficient guard will be invariably left in charge of the horses.

3. The men fall in to mount at the word "*Stand to your Horses,*" followed by "*Attention.*" They are to front their horses' heads, holding each bridoon rein near the ring, and at the word "*Prepare to mount,*" each man unlinks his horse, and puts the chain or rein over the horse's neck to the off side, the rights and lefts of Threes rein back their horses to the stated distance, and the whole step in to their horses, proceed with the usual motions in the manner directed, and, when mounted, fasten the collar rein or chain.

4. Should the Files, on any occasion of dismounting, be doubled up without the horses being linked, the above instructions with regard to mounting will apply, excepting that the men fall in, fronting the same way with their horses, and that at the word "*Prepare to Mount*" the rights and lefts step forward, face their horses, and rein them back into their places.

Section XXII. DISMOUNTED SERVICE.

1. "*With Carbines, Prepare to Dismount.*" The Front rank advances a horse's length and halts; after a moment's pause, the "Centres" of Threes, of both ranks, move forward a horse's length, and the "Rights of Threes" ease off half a yard to the left, for room to dismount. The "Rights" and "Lefts" of Threes swivel their carbines*, and (having undone the straps) shift them to the near side.

2. "*Dismount.*" The "Rights" and "Lefts" of Threes dismount, and leading up their horses, give them to the "Centres," and then hook or strap up their swords. During the time they remain dismounted, their carbines are not to be unswivelled.

3. "*Front Form, Quick March.*" The front rank men move on in quick time, with arms at the trail, and close in to the centre of the Squadron; the rear rank, facing outwards from the centre, file in double quick time, with trailed arms, round the flanks of the front-rank horses, and form at one yard distance behind the front-rank men. The Squadron will then be ordered to "*Halt.*"

4. In Regiments having Standards, the Non-commissioned Officer who carries the Standard remains mounted, as also his Coverer.

5. The Squadron and Troop Leaders command the dismounted men in the same way as when mounted. When the firing commences, they will take post according to regulation. The Squadron and Troop Serrefiles remain in charge of the led horses. The Squadron Marker comes to the front and holds the horse of the Squadron Leader. The Troop Serrefiles take the horses of the Troop Leaders.

6. It must be a rule, when a Squadron dismounts to act on foot, to protect the horses either by a Mounted Squadron or Troop.

---

* The directions as to the swivelling and securing the Carbine are here laid down as in the Regulars, but with the short Yeomanry Carbine, now in preparation, it will be found far the best to carry that arm in a holster behind the right thigh, as adopted already by several corps of Yeomanry.

7. On the word "*Quick March*," the Squadron advances for a short distance, and the Squadron Leader gives the word, "*Right*, or *Left*" } *Troop, Extend to Skirmish;*" on which the centre Files of that Troop continuing to move straight forward, the remainder incline outwards, and move on in double time, each File turning to the front again, and resuming the quick march as soon as it has got its distance, which should be about eight paces. The rear rank of the Skirmishers should drop behind their front rank, and follow at a distance of thirty paces; observing that this distance, as well as that between the Files, must entirely depend on the nature of the ground, and must be less in thickets and brushwood. The supporting Troop is halted by its Leader till the Skirmishers have gone forward one hundred paces, and then receiving from him the word "*Quick March*," follows in conformity to the movements of the Skirmishers.

8. When the Skirmishers receive from their Troop Leader the word "*Commence Firing*," the front-rank man of each File kneels and fires independently with a deliberate aim, and then loads his carbine as quickly as possible. The rear rank instantly runs forward twenty paces beyond the front rank, and fires in the same way, observing, however, as a rule, that no man must fire till his comrade behind him is loaded, and has given him the word "*Ready*" in a low voice.

9. When the whole are to retire, the Squadron Leader gives the word "*About*," repeated by Troop Leaders. If there has been any command to "*Cease Firing*," the Skirmishers face about, and retire in the same order as they happened to be standing; but if there has been no such command, they retire by alternate ranks, firing, the same as when advancing, taking care that both ranks are never unloaded at the same time. The men of the rank which has fired last must not begin loading until they have passed the rank behind them; because it is always an object to clear the front quickly for the rank which is loaded.

10. When the supporting Troop has retired to within thirty yards of the horses, it halts, fronts, and waits the arrival of the

DISMOUNTED SERVICE.

Skirmishers, who close in as they retire, and form upon the support. The whole are faced to the right-about, retire in quick time, and receive the word "*File to your Horses;*" the Rear rank then turning outwards move in double quick time, and the whole run at once to the front of their horses, and take the reins from their centre men, who then move forward a horse's length, and the others unhook their swords and stand ready to mount; the "Right" of Threes having inclined their horses half a yard to the left, to get room for the purpose.

11. "*Mount.*" The "Rights" and "Lefts" of Threes mount their horses, and dress up to the "Centres;" the rear rank takes close order, and the men who have been dismounted strap and unswivel their carbines. It may sometimes be expedient for the Support and Skirmishers to mount without any previous halt or formation, which must be effected as expeditiously as possible.

12. Dismounted Skirmishers and Supports act upon the word "*Right* (or *Left*) *incline*," when required to gain ground to either flank. When they are to halt, the whole kneel or lie down, according to circumstances.

13. Every man should be instructed to take advantage of the shelter of bushes, trees, ditches, &c., without too much regard to the regularity of dressing or interval, the front and rear rank of each File being accustomed to act in concert, and protect each other, by alternate loading and firing.

14. To attack a bridge or narrow pass, the men of the skirmishing Troop close inwards as they approach it, and run on quickly upon the point of attack, while the supporting Troop extends and opens a fire along the banks of the stream or flanks of the defile, to cover their advance; or else follows closely in a compact body, should the ground not admit of its fire being useful. The moment the Skirmishers have cleared the defile, they extend as before.

15. To retire through a pass, or over a bridge, the supporting Troop retreats first, and then extends to cover by its fire the retreat of the Skirmishers, who take care not to close until very

near the bridge or narrow passage. As soon as all have gone past, the Skirmishers extend as before, and the Support closes and acts in reserve.

OBSERVATIONS. It may be well to explain that the instructions in this Section are by no means intended to be applied to Regimental Movement. The object is merely to enable a Squadron, Troop, or any smaller Detachment, to act with readiness and effect, where their horses could not go; and the duties of Yeomanry, when in aid of the civil power, make it very essential that they should be perfectly efficient for forcing their way into inclosures or buildings, for the dispersion or capture of Rioters who may have taken advantage of such shelter. Occasions may also occur of hollow roads being blocked up, or so defended by a very few people as to make it absolutely necessary to clear a passage by a dismounted party, before it would be prudent to move forward mounted.

It is a most useful practice for a Troop of Yeomanry occasionally to dismount, and occupy a building or farm-yard, with reference to its defence. In distributing the men to their posts, care should be taken to explain the nature of a flanking fire, and other means by which a small number of men, skilfully distributed, can assume a formidable attitude in the protection and defence of houses, factories, or other property. A little consideration directed to this subject will enable any intelligent person to make himself acquainted with the chief points in question, and they may sometimes be of great importance to the Yeomanry Officer.

PART THE THIRD.

FIELD MOVEMENTS,

ETC.

Fig. A.
Regiment in Line.

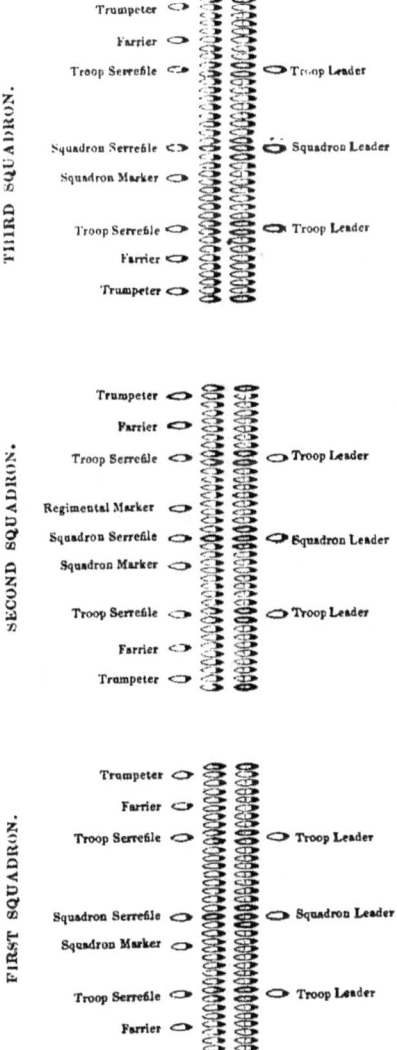

Fig. B.

The Regiment in Close Column of Squadrons,
Right in Front.

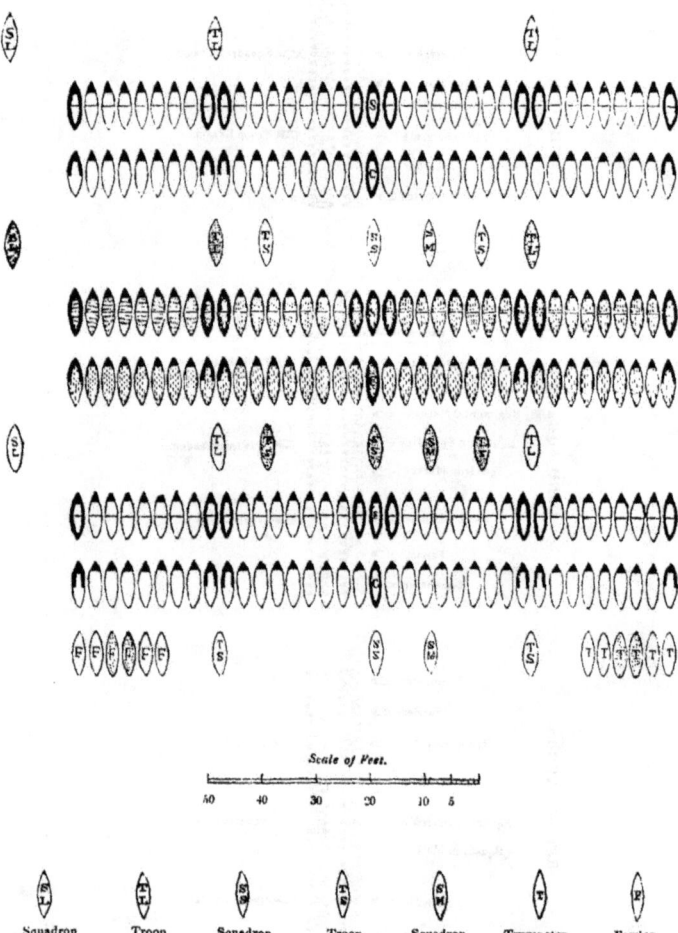

Fig. C   103

The Regiment in Open Column of Troops,
Right in Front.

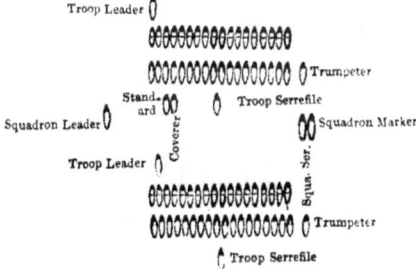

FIRST SQUADRON.

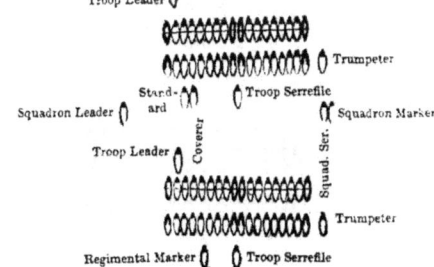

SECOND SQUADRON.

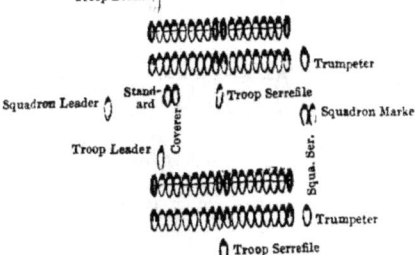

THIRD SQUADRON.

Fig. D.

Squadron of Forty-eight Files in open Column of Divisions, Right in Front.

Scale of Feet.

Note.—If the Squadron is the leading one of a Column, the Right Troop Leader rides in front of the Pivot Guide.

Fig. E.

Squadron of Thirty six Files in Column of Divisions, Right in Front.

Fig. F.

Squadron of Thirty-six Files in Column of Threes, Right in Front.

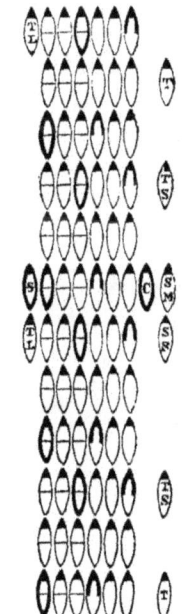

Scale of Feet.

Section I.

FORMATION OF THE REGIMENT.

The figs. A, B, C, show the Formation of a Regiment in Line, in Close Column, and in Open Column of Troops. Figs. D, E, F, show the Formation of Columns of Divisions and Threes.

Section II.

POST AND DUTIES OF OFFICERS.

1. In Line, the Squadron Leader is in front of the centre of his Squadron; the Squadron Serrefile in rear of it; Troop Leaders in front of the centre of their Troops; Troop Serrefiles in rear of them. (See fig. A.)

When retiring in Line the Serrefile Officers lead, but do not give the words of command.

2. In Open Column of Squadrons, the Squadron Leaders are in line with the Troop Leaders, and at two horses' lengths from the flank of the Column.

3. In Close Column of Squadrons, the Squadron Leaders are at a horse's length from the pivot flank, and in line with the Troop Leaders. The Troop Leaders are in front of the centre of their Troops; the Serrefiles in rear of them, on the same alignment as the Troop Leaders of the next Squadron, at half a horse's length from each, towards the centre of the Column. The Adjutant, covered by the Regimental Marker, is to be on the reverse flank of the Squadron at the head of the Column. (See fig. B.)

4. When a Close Column takes ground to its pivot flank, Squadron Leaders conduct the Heads of their Squadrons in front

of the leading Threes; but when it takes ground to its reverse hand they do not shift to the reverse flank to lead, and the Heads of the Squadrons are then conducted by the Troop Leaders on the flanks of their leading Threes.

5. When a Squadron wheels Threes Right or Left to deploy, the Troop Leaders move up to the pivot flank of their leading Threes, resuming their usual posts when the Squadron is fronted to march up into Line.

6. The Squadron Leader, when Threes are wheeled to deploy, moves up to the side of the Leader of the headmost Troop; on the word "*March*" he proceeds with his Squadron, but halts himself when opposite where the inward flank will stand in Line, until he judges the leading Threes have got their distance; he then gives the word "*Halt, Front, Forward*," hastening to the centre to lead his Squadron up into Line.

7. When, for any particular occasion, a Close Column is formed of Troops, the Troop Leaders are half a horse's length from the flank of the pivot File, in line with the front rank; each Squadron Leader at a horse's length interval from the Officer of his leading Troop; the Serrefiles on the reverse flank.

8. In the Open Column and Oblique Echellon of Troops, the Squadron Leader superintends the movements of both his Troops; Troop Leaders are in front of the second File from the pivot or directing flank, to which point they move, on the completion of the wheel from Line into Column (see fig. c) or Echellon.

9. In similar movements by Divisions, Troop Leaders take post in the same manner in front of the second File from the pivot or directing flank of the first and fourth Divisions (see fig. D); but when the Squadron is marching by Divisions of less than twelve Files for Column of Route, Troop Leaders are on the pivot flanks of the leading Divisions of their Troops. (See fig. E.)

10. When marching in Open Column, the Troop Leaders are answerable for their distances. The Troop Guides are

answerable for their covering, and for preserving the proper distance of front ranks from Troop Leaders. Squadron Leaders superintend the whole, and the Squadron Leader at the head of the Column is answerable that the Pivot Guide of the leading Troop marches steadily in the true direction.

11. When retiring in Open Column or Oblique Echellon of Troops, by " Threes About," Troop Serrefiles lead in front of the second File, and attend to their distances; but the words of command still proceed from the Troop Leaders. The Pivot Guide of each Troop turns about (outwards) and rides on the flank of his rear-rank.

12. In Movements by Threes, each Troop Leader is on the pivot flank of his leading Threes (see fig. F), except when an Open Column of Troops takes ground to its flank, on which occasion he leads in front of the pivot of his leading Threes.

13. When marching by Files, the Troop Leader is on the pivot flank of his leading Files.

14. The Squadron Leader, in all cases where his post is not specially laid down, moves wherever he can best superintend his men, and can best be heard by them.

Section III. COMMANDS.

1. ALL Commands must be given in a firm, loud, and clear tone; every Officer must therefore be accustomed to give such commands, even to small bodies, loud enough not only to be heard by such bodies as are immediately under his orders, but also by the Leaders of others who are dependent on his motions.

2. The Commanding Officer gives the general caution, which is immediately repeated by the Squadron Leaders*, who then proceed to give the preparatory words necessary for executing the Movement indicated. When those words have been given,

---

* When a Regiment is in Close Column, the general commands given by the Commanding Officer are not repeated by Squadron Leaders.

the Commanding Officer directs the Trumpet to sound the pace at which the Movement is to be made; the Squadron Leaders announce the pace as a caution, by the word "*Walk, Trot,* or *Gallop,*" and the executive word "*March,*" from the Commanding Officer, (repeated, quickly and distinctly, by the Squadron Leaders,) puts the whole into motion.

3. When the Troops composing a Squadron are to move or wheel in the same manner and at the same time, the command is given by the Squadron Leader; but when differently or successively, the command is given by each Troop Leader.

4. When a general order is not distinctly heard by a part of the Line, each Squadron Leader (when the intention is obvious) will conform as quickly as possible to the Movement which he sees executed on his right or left, according to the point from whence he perceives it to begin.

5. It is not sufficient for a Commanding Officer to give his word of command correctly; but the moment he has uttered his caution, he should give his attention to the Squadron Leaders' repetition of it; and if he perceives that any one has either misunderstood, or not heard it, he should repeat it loudly and clearly. He will thus make sure of his word of execution taking effect at once, when he gives it; and so far from any loss of time, the steady and uniform performance of the Movement will far more than compensate for the first delay.

Section IV.

PRINCIPLES OF FIELD MOVEMENT.

1. All wheels of the Squadron, Troop, or Division, from the Halt (unless otherwise ordered), are to be made at the rate of the Trot of manœuvre.

2. After wheels of a body previously in movement, the former rate of march will be resumed at the word "*Forward.*"

3. The centre Squadron, or (if the numbers be even) the right centre Squadron, whether the Line consist of one or more Regiments, is to be the Squadron of Direction, unless any other Squadron is specially named by the Commanding Officer.

4. The change of direction in Echellon Formations is always made by the word "*Right*" or "*Left*" for the degree of wheel required, followed by the word "*Forward,*" as soon as the Troop is parallel to the New Line.

5. The Changes of Front in Line are executed by the Echellon March of Troops, either to the front or rear.

6. Changes of Front of a less degree than one eighth of the circle are to be made on the Base, by the Squadrons moving entire, as laid down in the observations on Movement No. VI. from Line (p. 139).

7. Changes of Position of the Regiment from one distant situation to another are made either in Line, by the direct Echellon, by the oblique Echellon of Troops, by Squadron Columns of Threes or Division, or by the movements of the Open Column.

8. In Changes of Position by Oblique Echellon the Troops wheel half the amount of the intended change, then move to the new Position, where the Base Troop again wheels the required degree into the new Alignment, and the Formation is completed in the usual manner.

9. Distant Positions, where circumstances will allow, are easiest and soonest taken by the March of the Open Column.

For this purpose the whole Line wheels to the hand ordered, by Troops or Divisions, and moves off in a general Column.

10. The Changes of Front and Position by Oblique Echellon are almost equal in security to the march of the Regiment in front, or to a uniform wheel of the Line; they can be used in the most critical situations, where the movements of the Open Column could not be risked. The advantages attending them are, the preserving a general front during the March, and enabling a Body to change Front or Position either on a fixed or moving point, retaining the power at any moment to stop the movement and form a line.

11. INVERSION. Although Inversion of the Line should generally be avoided, yet situations will occur where it is indispensable, and it therefore cannot be neglected in practice.

For instance, a Column with its Right in front may arrive on the left of its ground, and be obliged immediately to form up, and support that point, so that the Right of the Line will become the Left (see Movement No. XII. from Open Column), or it may be necessary for a Column to form Line to its reverse flank as nearly as possible upon its own ground (see Movement No XI. from Open Column).

But on the whole it is to be recollected, that though the Inversion of Squadrons in a Regiment, ought to create no real inconvenience, yet, that of the Troops or Divisions of the Squadron within itself would lead to disorder, and is on all occasions to be avoided.

12. Cavalry acting with Infantry, and required to advance, can pass through the Infantry Line either in Open Columns of Troops, or Squadron Columns of Divisions, or Threes, or can advance round the flanks in Single or Double Columns of Troops, forming their line as they move forward.

13. When Cavalry are to withdraw to the rear of a Line of Infantry, they should retire in Open Column of Troops round one or both flanks of the Infantry, so as to clear their front quickly, and allow of their opening their fire.

14. When Infantry are thrown into Squares, Cavalry can always retire between them in Squadron Columns of Threes, because there is then no risk of deranging their order.

Section V.

RULES FOR MARKERS AND DRESSING.

1. The Markers to be employed for Regimental Movements are the Adjutant, the Regimental Serjeant-Major, and one Non-commissioned Officer for each Squadron. ~~The Troop Leader~~ of the Base Troop is ~~on all occasions~~ employed ~~to mark the Base of the intended Line~~, and is placed by the Squadron Leader.

2. ~~In all dressing in Line~~ the Squadron and Troop Leaders will face their Squadrons, and the Alignment will be taken up within half a foot of their horses' heads. When the dressing is completed, the word "*Eyes Front*" is given, and the Officers resume their posts half a horse's length in front of their Squadrons*.

3. When a correction of dressing after an Advance in Line is required, the Troop Leaders of the Squadron of Direction are directed to raise their swords for the Base (but without turning their horses about) on the Alignment on which they stand, and the Commanding Officer gives the word "*On the Alignment, Dress*," which is rapidly taken up along the Line.

4. When a Division, Troop, or Squadron, is merely to correct its dressing by its own directing flank, the word "*Dress*" is employed; but when it is to move up bodily, and take up its dressing from a previously formed Line, the command to be given is "*Dress up;*" for instance, when an Open Column forms line on its leading Troop, that Troop, after advancing the prescribed three horses' lengths, is halted, and receives the word "*Dress*," but the remaining Troops, successively halting short of the Alignment, are moved up to it by the command "*Dress up.*"

---

* It is strongly recommended to Yeomanry to simplify this rule, by the men taking up the Alignment at half a horse's length from the heads of the Officers' and Markers' horses, instead of at half a foot; so that on the on the word "*Eyes Front*," the Officers will only have to turn their own horses about, exactly where they stand, without any subsequent dressing forward, which always causes a degree of unsteadiness.

5. In successive Formations of Line, each Squadron Leader gives the word "*Eyes front*," as soon as his own Squadron is properly dressed, and the Officers of the next are arrived upon the Alignment*; upon this word the Officers front, and move up to their posts at half a horse's length from the Ranks; the Marker goes to the rear, and the men look to their front; but the Base Officer and Marker invariably remain posted until the whole Regiment is formed. In case of the first formed Squadron being required to act immediately, as may sometimes occur on service, the next Squadron gives the Base for those not yet arrived on the Line.

6. Officers and Markers employed in giving Bases for Lines, raise the hilts of their swords to the height of the cheek, keeping the blade perfectly upright, and with the edge to the front. Markers for the covering of Columns turn the edge sideways.

7. A Marker should in general move out from his Squadron just time enough to take his dressing from the Base, before the Squadron arrives on the Line.

8. In Changes of Front from Line, and in Formations of Line from Open Column, the Base consists of the Leader of the Base Troop, and the Marker of the Squadron to which that Troop belongs. This Marker, immediately upon the Caution, places himself, with his sword raised, facing to where the flank File of the Base Troop will stand after it shall have wheeled or moved up; and the Leader of that Troop quits his post the moment he has given the preparatory command to his Troop to wheel or move up, and places himself, with his sword raised, facing to where the centre of his Troop will arrive. Both he and the Marker remain fixed till the Regiment is formed. The Leader of the Squadron, from which the Base is thus given, goes to the outside of the Base, the moment he has repeated the Caution, to see that it is in its proper direction. Having corrected it, if necessary, he places himself quickly in line with it, facing to where the centre of his Squadron will arrive. Meantime the Major or Adjutant rides, immediately upon the Caution, to

---

* See the Note to Art. 2.

MARKERS AND DRESSING.

the Base placed by the Leader of the Squadron from which it is given, and sees that the Leaders of the other Squadrons and Troops dress correctly upon it as they arrive in line. The Markers of all but the Base Squadron take up the outer points as their Squadrons approach the Line; each remains stationary till his Squadron is dressed, and goes to the rear immediately that the Squadron Leader gives the word "*Eyes Front.*"

9. In forming Close Column, the Base for the Covering consists of the Marker of that Squadron on which the Formation takes place, and the Serjeant-Major; who are placed by the Adjutant, immediately upon the Caution, facing to the pivot flank of the intended Column.

10. In Deployments, and all other movements from Close Column, the Base consists of the Regimental Marker and the Marker of that Squadron upon which the Deployment or the Movement takes place, who are placed by the Adjutant, immediately upon the Caution, at one horse's length from the head of the Column.

11. In a Deployment a Marker should arrive at his post about forty yards in advance of his Squadron, so as to be steadily aligned on the Base before it reaches him.

12. When a Regiment in Open Column enters a distant Position, the Adjutant marks the point of entry.

13. When a Column changes its direction, the Adjutant marks the point where such Change is made. If the Changes are frequent, the Serjeant-Major is to assist him.

14. When a Line is ordered to "*Change Front*" on a flank, no Troop or Squadron is to be named in the Caution, but such change is to be made on the flank Troop of the Line, which will give the Base accordingly.

15. In Changes of Front on a central part of the Line, the particular Squadron must be indicated; and it is then understood that if the Change of Front is to the right, the right Troop, but if to the left, the left Troop, of that Squadron gives the Base.

MARKERS AND DRESSING.

16. In Formations of Line on a central part of an Open Column, the intended Squadron must be named in the Caution; and if the Formation is to the front, the leading Troop, but if to the rear, the rear Troop, of the named Squadron gives the Base.

17. When a Brigade changes its front or forms Line from Open Column, the Base given by the Troop on which the Change or Formation takes place, serves as the general Base for the whole Line, but as soon as the first Squadron of the next Regiment has arrived and formed on the Line, the Base Officer and Marker drop their swords and return to their usual places.

18. When a Brigade assembles in Contiguous Column, the inward flank of each Regiment is marked by its Serjeant-Major, who is posted by an Officer of the General's Staff.

19. When the Caution is given for a Brigade to deploy on one of the Squadrons of a central or rear Regiment, Commanding Officers are answerable for immediately sending up to the head of the Column, ~~the two Markers for the Base Squadron and also the Marker for the Squadron next in front of it, who are then posted by an Officer of the General's Staff.~~

Section VI.

TAKING UP POINTS OF FORMATION.

The general direction of the Alignment upon which a Column is to form must always be considered before entering upon it, two objects in nature being usually determined as points of direction for the extremities of the intended Line.

If the Column is to enter the Alignment at one of those objects, no difficulty occurs in there placing the Base pointing upon the other more distant object; but if the Column is to enter the intended Alignment at any central or intermediate point, or if, as may often be the case, the objects which have been determined as a guidance for the direction of the Line are distant or inaccessible, the Alignment in which the Base is to be placed for the Formation to commence must be ascertained by the following method, in which Officers and Non-commissioned Officers should be frequently practised.

Suppose the mill and the steeple, are two distant or inaccessible objects, between which a column is to enter, in order to deploy or form Line in any other manner. The two objects in question are pointed out to two Officers or Non-commissioned

118   POINTS OF FORMATION.

Officers, A and B, usually the Adjutant and Serjeant-Major. A chooses one of the objects (suppose the mill) as his regulating point, and places himself with his side towards it, and his horse's head towards the intended Alignment.

B instantly posts himself about fifty yards from A, on that side of him which is farthest from the mill, with his horse's head also towards the intended Alignment, and dresses himself exactly upon A and the mill.

As soon as he has placed himself correctly as described, he gives the word "*Ready*," upon which they both start, A riding straight forward at a steady canter towards where the head of the Column is to follow, occasionally glancing his eye towards the Steeple; and B riding a certain degree faster so as to keep the mill still exactly in a line with A as he advances, and at the same time preserving his fifty yards' distance from his flank.

As they thus approach the intended Alignment, A must begin to fix his eye upon the steeple, and also to observe B as he appears coming into line with it, gradually slackening his own pace to a walk, to allow of B keeping his dressing more steadily.

The moment he sees B come into line with the steeple, he stops his horse, giving him the word "*Halt*," and raising his sword. B, halting instantly, likewise raises his sword, both turn their horses quietly to the right-about, and the points are thus established, upon which the advancing Column is enabled to place its own Base in the usual manner, and proceed with its Formation or Deployment. Where there are more Regiments than one, the above method will be observed for the Regiment of direction, the Adjutants of the other Regiments arriving in succession, and placing themselves as the Points of Entry in prolongation of the Base thus given.

Section VII.

MARCH IN LINE, DIRECTION, AND ALIGNMENT.

The March of the Line in front is the most difficult and most important of all movements.

1. When marching in Line, the men of each Squadron dress to their centre, and the Squadron Leaders line with and preserve their intervals from each other, and the Squadron of Direction; but with as much reference as possible to that Squadron. The Leader of the Squadron of Direction takes a point in the distance perpendicular to his front, and selects intermediate objects upon which he is to move. Both the Troop Leaders of the Squadron of Direction take post in front of the third Files from the Flanks during the advance, and raise their swords in order to furnish a Base for the ~~whole line of Officers~~.

2. One of the Troop Leaders of the Squadron of Direction regulates the Base of the Alignment. In the advance he must endeavour to keep this Base square and parallel to the original Alignment, by increasing or slackening his pace as he sees occasion. The other Troop Leader conforms, by keeping himself dressed on the Squadron Leader and the Officer of Alignment.

3. If the First, Central, or any intermediate Squadron is the one of Direction, the Right Troop Leader of that Squadron is the Officer of Alignment; if on the left of the centre, the Left Troop Leader. The Major or Adjutant superintends the Officer of Alignment.

4. It is an essential rule for all other Squadrons to be, if anything, rather behind the Squadron of direction in advancing in line.

5. When a change of direction is to be given to an advancing Line, the Officer of Alignment will increase or slacken his pace according to the instructions he receives; the Leader of the Squadron of Direction will gradually circle into the new direction, the other Troop Leader conforming to the change, and the Leaders of the other Squadrons gradually taking up the new dressing. When the desired alteration is made in the direction of the advancing Line, the word "*Forward*" is given.

MARCH IN LINE, DIRECTION, AND ALIGNMENT.

6. Inclining is the method by which the Line gains ground to the flank, without altering its parallel direction. At the word *"Forward"* it resumes its direct advance. During the incline, the Flank Squadron, on the hand to which the incline is made, becomes the Squadron of Direction.

7. When parts of the Line are impeded by any inequalities of the ground, or other obstacle, they are to be passed with regularity and order, by filing from the Right of Threes,—by breaking into Files, Threes, or Divisions from the Right or Left of Squadrons, or by doubling Squadrons, Troops, or Divisions, into Column, each body reforming as soon as clear. No Exercise is more important or requires greater practice.

8. When there is sufficient extent of ground, it should be a frequent practice to make long Advances in Line, changing the direction of the Line, inclining and again advancing, occasionally altering the pace by increasing it from the walk to the gallop, and again decreasing it from the gallop to the walk by gradual degrees.

9. As a general rule, almost every movement at a Field Day should be followed by an Advance in Line.

10. After the March in Line, on the word *"Halt,"* each Squadron halts and dresses by its centre; their Leaders by the Squadron of Direction: and if the dressing of the general Line is to be afterwards corrected, it ought to begin at, and be taken up from, the Squadron of Direction.

11. Where the whole Line is to be new dressed, and where circumstances admit, much facility attends the operation, if such an Alignment is taken as causes a dressing forward, however small, of every Squadron that composes it.

12. If the Squadron intervals are false in the centre of a Line, they must remain so till corrected by order, and by a separate operation of flank marching; but the Leader of a Flank Squadron should never lose a moment in correcting his interval, if false, because its correction does not interfere with any other part of the Line.

In the Retreat of the Line the same rules apply as in the Advance, the Squadron Serrefiles acting as Leaders.

Section VIII. FORMATION FOR ATTACK.

1. The formation of a body of Cavalry for an Attack depends much upon the opposition to be expected, and also upon the nature of the ground; which should be reconnoitred (when it is practicable) to the Front and Flanks.

2. The Force should be formed in three distinct bodies, distinguished as "First Line," "Support," and "Reserve."

The "First Line" should seldom consist of more than one-third of the whole Force; it should be formed in Line.

The "Support" may be either in Line, or in Columns.

The "Reserve" should be in similar Columns.

3. The distance from the "First Line" to the "Support," as well as from the "Support" to the "Reserve," must be sufficient to preserve the "Support" from being disordered, should the "First Line," be forced to retreat; in no case less than 200 yards.

4. The "Support" and the "Reserve" must steadily follow the advance of the "First Line," maintaining their respective distances; but the moment the "First Line" is seen commencing its charge, they must both draw up to a walk, and continue at that pace till the evident success of the "First Line" warrants their more rapid advance, or till (in the event of its failure) it has retired, and cleared the front of the "Support," so as to enable the latter to attack with full effect, and probably convert the failure of the "First Line" into success; but for this it is essential that the Officers of the "First Line" should use every exertion to get their men away round the Flanks, and rally them behind the "Reserve," instead of their falling back upon the "Support," and destroying the steadiness, and order, of its attack.

Section IX. THE CHARGE OR ATTACK.

1. The great force of Cavalry is more in the offensive than the defensive; therefore, the Attack is its principal object.

2. All the different movements of the Line should tend to place it in the most advantageous situation for attack.

3. When the Line is to Charge, the words of command are "*March!*" "*Trot!*" "*Gallop!*" "*Charge!*" "*Walk!*" and "*Halt!*"

4. The Commanding Officer should lead at such a pace as that the flanks and rear rank may always keep up; but, at the same time, it is most essential that the flanks should not press before the centre. Every alteration of pace must be made as gradually as possible, and at the same instant, by the whole Line.

5. Whatever distance a Line has to go over, it is desirable, if the nature of the ground will permit, that it should move at a steady trot till within two hundred yards, and then gallop, making a progressive increase, till within forty or fifty yards of the point of attack, when the word "*Charge*" will be given, and the gallop made with as much rapidity as the body can bear in good order. Of course the distances here laid down must in many cases be left to the discretion of the Commanding Officer, and are only meant for general guidance at ordinary Field Days.

6. It is from the uniform velocity of a Line that its greatest effect is to be derived; it must, therefore, on no account, be so much hurried as to bring up the horses blown, or even distressed, to the attack.

7. In every part of the Charge, and in quick movement, the centre of each Squadron must be very exact in following the Leader, and the men particularly attentive in keeping up to, and dressing to, their centre, without closing or opening their distance, and taking care that the flanks are not too forward. They should have their horses in hand, and perfectly square to

CHARGE OR ATTACK.

the front, with their heads well up, which will keep them under command.

8. After a Charge or Attack of any description, the great object of the Officers and Non-commissioned Officers should be to restore order, and form Line as steadily and quickly as possible.

9. If the Line fails in its attack, Officers must endeavour to prevent their men from falling back on their Support. They must try to lead them round its flanks, and rally them in the rear. Nothing can be more fatal than a disordered body throwing itself back upon a Line advancing to its assistance.

10. In the real Charge, the halt of the Line depends upon the nature of the resistance which is met with; in ordinary exercise, after the Charge, the word "*Walk*" will be given, when the pace will be gradually decreased, and a distance of thirty or forty yards will be allowed before the final "*Halt.*"

11. There can be no occasion on which it is eligible for Cavalry to wait and receive the attack. Though circumstances of situation may prevent a Line from advancing much, it should never absolutely stand still to receive an attack; otherwise its defeat is almost inevitable.

12. In the Advance in Line the Sword will be carried; in the Charge it will be brought to the "Engage," (by the front rank only,) and, on the order to "*Walk*," it will be sloped.

Section X.

INSPECTION OR REVIEW OF THE REGIMENT.

Formation of the Regiment for Parade Movements.

The figure A shows the Formation of the Regiment.

1. The Commanding Officer takes post two horses' lengths in front of the Leader of the Centre Squadron. The other Field Officers are a horse's length before the Leaders of the Flank Squadrons, but during the movements they assist in the field, by superintending the bases and dressing, commanding second Lines, or directing detached Squadrons, Advanced Guards, &c.

2. The Adjutant and Staff in one rank on the right of the Regiment, at a horse's length interval from it, dressing by the front rank; the Band or Trumpeters in two or more ranks on the right of the Staff, and at a like interval.

3. The Regiment being formed on the ground where the Reviewing-Officer is to be received, a point is to be marked about 150 or 200 yards in front of the centre, at which the Officer is expected to take his station, and that spot is to be considered the point to work upon.

4. The Regiment takes order in the manner prescribed in Part II., Sect. XII., p. 68, the Officers and rear rank dressing by the Squadron of Direction.

5. When the Reviewing Officer presents himself before the centre, the words "*Eyes right—Draw Swords*," are given; the Officers coming down at the last motion to the position of the salute; the Standards salute such persons only, as, from Rank and Regulation, are entitled to that honour; the Band plays, or Trumpets sound, according to the rank of the Reviewing Officer; after which the Officers recover their swords with the Commanding Officer.

MARCHING PAST.

6. The Reviewing Officer then goes towards the right, accompanied by the Commanding Officer, and the whole remain steady while he passes along the Regiment, during which time the Band will play, or Trumpets sound.

7. When the Reviewing Officer is proceeding to place himself in the front, the Commanding Officer orders "*Rear Rank, take Close Order—March.*" On this particular occasion the Officers and Standard remain as at order.

Marching Past.

8. When the Caution is given to "*March past by Squadrons,*" the Adjutant marks the passing line by placing the Marker of the Second Squadron at point B, about forty yards on the right

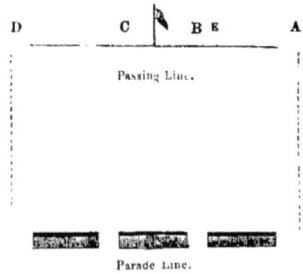

of the centre facing the Regiment, and on a line about four yards in advance of that upon which the Reviewing Officer is supposed to take post. The Regimental Sergeant-Major places himself at C, at an equal distance on the left of the centre, dressing by the Marker of the Second Squadron and the Adjutant, who posts himself at E, about twelve yards beyond that Marker, until the Serjeant-Major has placed himself correctly.

9. The Markers of the First and Third (or Fourth) Squadrons ride out to the front, halt and turn about, when they arrive at A and D, each outflanking the Regiment by about twenty yards, and dress by the Serjeant-Major and Marker of the Second Squadron.

10. On the word "*March past by Squadrons,*" repeated by Squadron Leaders, the latter (still remaining opposite the centres of their Squadrons) give the word "*Threes Right.*" On the word "*March,*" the Staff fall out; and as soon as the Column is in motion the Commanding Officer gives the word "*Slope Swords,*" the head of the Column receiving the words "*Left Wheel — Forward,*" when opposite the Marker, at A; and each Squadron, when its head arrives at the Passing Line, receiving the words "*Halt—Front—Forward,*" followed by "*Eyes Right.*" On arriving at B, the words are given "*Rear Rank, take Order—Carry Swords.*"

11. The Band is at a distance equal to the breadth of a Troop in front of the Column; and having passed the General, it wheels to its left, clears the flank of the Column, then wheels to the left about, and plays while the Regiment is passing.

12. The Officers being at the prescribed distance in front, salute when within ten yards of the Reviewing Officer, taking their time from the Commanding Officer and Squadron Leaders, and dress to the right. The Adjutant marches past two horses' lengths in rear of the third File from the pivot flank of the rear Squadron.

13. When the rear rank has passed the Reviewing Officer ten yards, Officers recover their swords with the Squadron Leaders.

14. On arriving at the Marker C, the words "*Rear Rank, take Close Order,*" and "*Slope Swords,*" are given, on which the Serrefile Officers take post in the rear.

15. Each Squadron, on reaching the point D of the Passing Line, receives the words "*Left Wheel—Forward.*"

16. As soon as the last Squadron has wheeled at the point D, the Commanding Officer gives the word "*Form Troops,*" upon which, the right Troop of each Squadron continuing its march, the left Troop receives from its Leader the words, "*Halt —Right Incline—March,*" followed by "*Forward*" as soon as it covers in Column. The word "*Trot*" is then given, and the

Column moves round the square, each Troop wheeling at the several angles, till the Leading Troop arrives within its own breadth of the commencement A, of the Passing Line, when the first Squadron receives from its Leader the word "*Left Wheel into Line,*" followed by "*Forward,*" and advances till within about ten yards of the point B; the word is then given "*Form Close Column;*" the first Squadron halts; the others, having successively wheeled into line the same as the first, move up to Close Column.

17. The Regiment will then rank past by Single Files*.

On the word "*Rank past by Single Files,*" the Right Troop Leader gives the word "*Carry Swords,*" "*From the left to the front rank off,*" "*March,*" and the Left Troop Leader, "*From the right to the front rank off,*" "*March,*" as it comes to his turn. Each Troop, preceded by its Officers according to seniority, ranks past from its inward flank; that is, the right Troops from their left, and the left Troops from their right, first all the front, and then all the rear rank. The Squadron Leader precedes the Leader of the right Troop; the Lieutenant-Colonel precedes the Regiment; and the Adjutant is in rear of the whole. Trumpeters rank past in front of the Officers; Farriers in rear of their Troops; Standards in rear of the Officers of the right Troops. Officers salute separately when ten yards from the General; Squadron Leaders, after having passed, fall out to the left, and front him while their respective Squadrons are passing.

18. Each Squadron forms on reaching D at the end of the Passing Line, and receives the word "*Slope Swords.*" It then wheels to the left, and advances sufficiently to allow the other Squadrons to form and wheel successively at D, and march up in Close Column behind it.

---

* This mode of filing past has always been followed in the Regulars, but to Yeomanry it is strongly recommended, instead of thus moving off from the inward flanks of Troops, to file past from the right of each Squadron, according to the ordinary method laid down, PART II. p. 72; thus avoiding a variety which is only for parade, and is liable to perplex the men in one of the most useful practices in their instruction.

19. As soon as the Close Column is thus formed, the caution is given "*Advance in ~~Open~~ Column of Troops from the Right.*" The right Troop of the first Squadron receives from its Leader the word "*Advance.*" On the words "*Trot*," "*March*," the right Troop advances, the left Troop receiving from its Leader "*Right, Incline, March*," as it gets room, and "*Forward*," when it covers the preceding Troop in Column. In the same manner the remaining Squadrons move successively into Open Column of Troops, (fig. c,) and trot round, each Troop receiving from its Leader the word "*Left Wheel*," followed by "*Forward*," at the angles.

20. On entering upon the Passing Line at A, Troop Leaders, after the wheel, take post in front of the second File from the Right, giving the words "*Eyes Right*," "*Carry Swords.*" Immediately before wheeling at D, they give the word "*Slope Swords:*" after the wheel, they resume their proper posts in front of the second File from the left, giving the word "*Eyes Left.*"

21. While upon the Passing Line the Squadron Leader precedes the Right Troop Leader, the Squadron Serrefile marches on a line with the right Troop Serrefile, in rear of the right flank of the right Troop. The Squadron Marker, if not wanted to mark the Passing Line, (as may happen when there is more than one Regiment,) marches in rear of the left flank of the left Troop, in line with the Serrefile. Troop Serrefiles are at their usual posts.

22. As soon as the rear of the Column has quitted the Passing Line, Markers rejoin their Squadrons.

23. The Troops having successively made a second wheel, the Column halts upon the original ground, and wheels into Line*.

24. When the Regiment begins to perform Field Movements, the Farriers and Band fall out; one Trumpeter remaining with

---

* Should the Sword Exercise be required, it is at this period it will be usually performed.

MARCHING PAST.

the Commanding Officer, and one with each Squadron, to repeat the soundings*.

25. At the conclusion of a Review, the Regiment or Line advances in Parade Order by the Squadron of Direction, opening the Ranks and carrying Swords on the march, and halting and saluting when within forty or fifty yards of the Reviewing Officer.

---

* Unless the Corps is provided with good Trumpeters, trained to horsemanship, and accustomed to Field-drill, it will be best to dispense with them in movement, and to trust to the voice alone.

FIELD MOVEMENTS.

In detailing the Field Movements, it has been deemed sufficient to lay them down as performed from the Right; to do them from the Left it will only be necessary to substitute, in the Cautions and Commands, the word *Left* for *Right*, and *Right* for *Left*.

Some few of the Movements laid down for the Regular Cavalry have been omitted as inapplicable to the Yeomanry Service, but it has been thought best to preserve the numbers by which the Movements are designated unaltered, and corresponding therefore with the Cavalry Regulations.

Unless with Corps of long standing and frequent assembly, it is strongly recommended to select the most necessary Movements only; and above all, not to attempt too many on occasions of Review.

Twelve or fourteen simple and useful Movements are quite enough for such occasions; and by repeating each two or three times over at preparatory Field-days, they will be well understood, and therefore well performed. Care should be taken, however, not to perform them always in the same order, but to consider each Movement as an independent exercise, otherwise the habit will be acquired of expecting the Movements to follow in a certain succession, which should of all things be avoided.

Section XI. MOVEMENTS FROM LINE.

Movement No. I. from Line.

Commanding Officer, repeated by Squadron Leaders, } "*Change Front, Half Right*.*"
Leader of the Base Troop, "*Right Troop, Half Right.*"
Leader of the Troop next the Base, "*Left Troop, Advance.*"
Leaders of the Second and Third Squadrons, } "*Troops Quarter Right.*"
Commanding Officer, repeated by Squadron Leaders, } { "*Walk,* or "*Trot,* } *March.*"

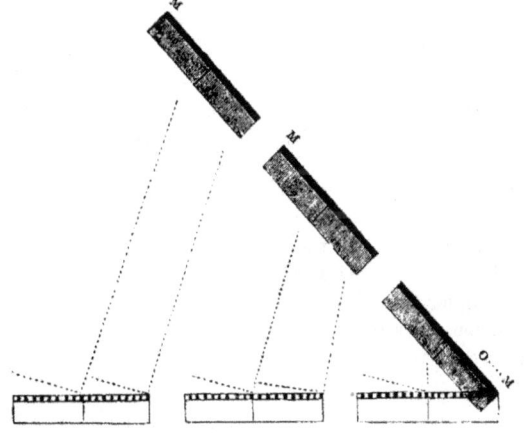

On the word "*March,*" the whole move as follows:

The Base Troop wheels half right, and receives from its Leader the words "*Halt, Dress.*"

The Troop next the Base advances till its right uncovers the left of the Base Troop: it then receives from its Leader the word "*Right,*" followed by "*Forward, Halt, Dress up.*"

The other Troops wheel quarter right, and then, receiving the word "*Forward*" from the Squadron Leaders, advance in echellon towards the new Line. Each, on approaching its place, receives from its Leader the word "*Right,*" followed by "*Forward,*" and on arriving on a line with the rear rank of the preceding Troop, "*Halt, Dress up.*"

---

* The Base is given by the Right Troop Leader and the Marker of the First Squadron.

Movement No. II. from Line.

Commanding Officer, repeated by Squadron Leaders, *"Change Front to the Right*."*

Leader of the Base Troop, *"Right Troop, Right Wheel."*

Leader of the Troop next the Base, *"Left Troop, Half Right."*

Leaders of the Second and Third Squadrons, *"Troops Half Right."*

Commanding Officer, repeated by Squadron Leaders, *"Walk,* or *Trot, March."*

On the word *"March,"* the Base Troop wheels to the right, and receives from its Leader the words *"Halt, Dress."*

The other Troops wheel half right, and then, receiving the word *"Forward"* from the Squadron Leaders, and the Leader of the Troop next the Base, advance in echellon, towards the new line, and form in the manner directed in No. I.

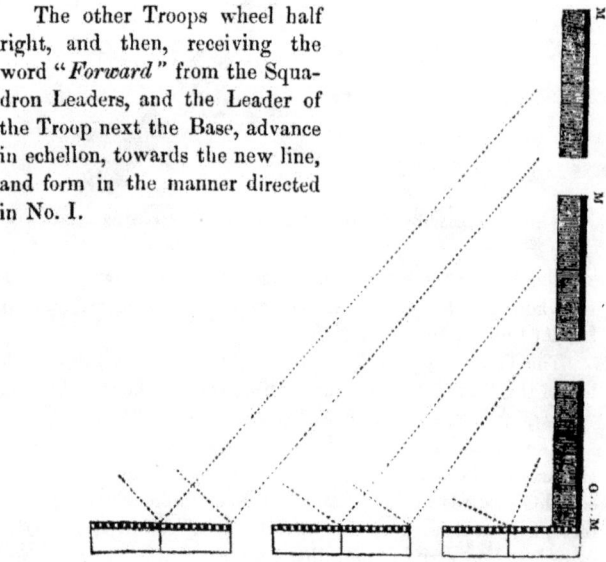

---

* The Base is given by the Right Troop Leader and the Marker of the First Squadron.

Movement No. III. from Line.

Commanding Officer, repeated by Squadron Leaders, } *"Change Front, Half Right, Back*."*

Leader of the Base Troop, *"Left Troop, Half Right."*

Leader of the Troop next the Base, *"Right Troop Threes about,"* followed by *"Half Right,"* as soon as the Threes have gone about.

Leaders of the First and Second Squadrons, *"Threes about,"* followed by *"Troops Quarter Right,"* as soon as the Threes have gone about.

Commanding Officer, repeated by Squadron Leaders, { *" Walk,* or *" Trot,* } *March."*

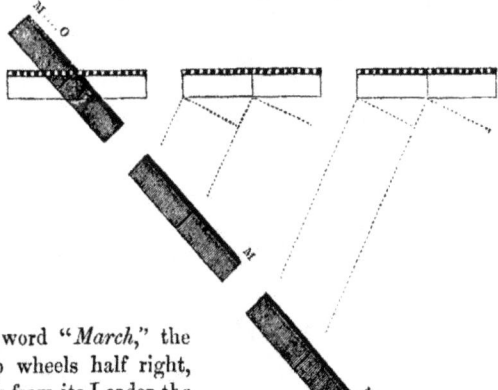

On the word *"March,"* the Base Troop wheels half right, and receives from its Leader the words *"Halt, Dress."*

The Troop next the Base wheels half right, receives from its Leader the word *"Forward;"* and when it has passed the line one horse's length, *"Halt, Front, Dress up."*

The other Troops wheel quarter right, and, receiving from the Squadron Leaders the word *"Forward,"* retire in echellon towards the new line. Each, on approaching its place, receives from its Leader the word *"Right,"* followed by *"Forward,"* and when it has passed the line one horse's length, *"Halt, Front, Dress up."*

---

* The Base is given by the Left Troop Leader and the Marker of the Third Squadron.

Movement No. IV. from Line.

Commanding Officer, repeated by Squadron Leaders, } "*Change Front, Right, Back*.*"

Leader of the Base Troop, "*Left Troop, Right Wheel.*"

Leader of the Troop next the Base, "*Right Troop, Threes about,*" followed by "*Right Wheel,*" as soon as the Threes have gone about.

Leaders of the First and Second Squadrons "*Threes about,*" followed by "*Troops Half Right,*" as soon as the Threes have gone about.

Commanding Officer, repeated by Squadron Leaders, { "*Walk,* or "*Trot,* } *March.*"

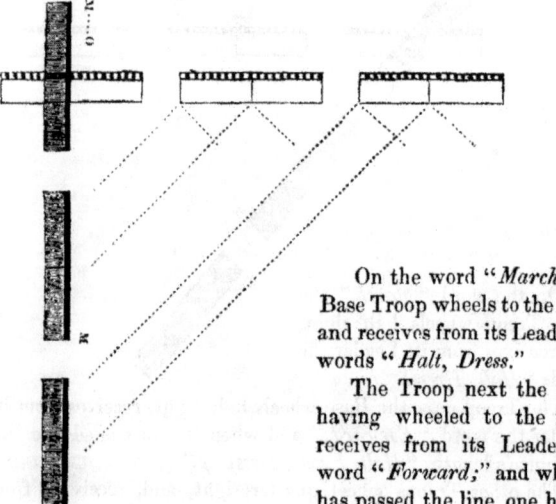

On the word "*March,*" the Base Troop wheels to the right, and receives from its Leader the words "*Halt, Dress.*"

The Troop next the Base, having wheeled to the right, receives from its Leader the word "*Forward;*" and when it has passed the line one horse's length, "*Halt, Front, Dress up.*"

The other Troops wheel half right, and receiving from the Squadron Leaders the word "*Forward,*" retire in echellon towards the new line, and form in the manner directed in No. III.

---

* The Base is given by the Left Troop Leader and the Marker of the Third Squadron.

Movement No. V. from Line.

Commanding Officer, repeated by Squadron Leaders, *"Change Front, Half Right, on the Second Squadron*."*

Leader of the Base Troop, *"Right Troop, Half Right."*

Leader of the First Squadron, *"Threes about,"* followed by *"Troops Quarter Right,"* as soon as the Threes have gone about.

Leader of the Troop next on the left of the Base, *"Left Troop, Advance."*

Leader of the Third Squadron, *"Troops Quarter Right."*

Commanding Officer, repeated by Squadron Leaders, *"Walk,"* or *"Trot, March."*

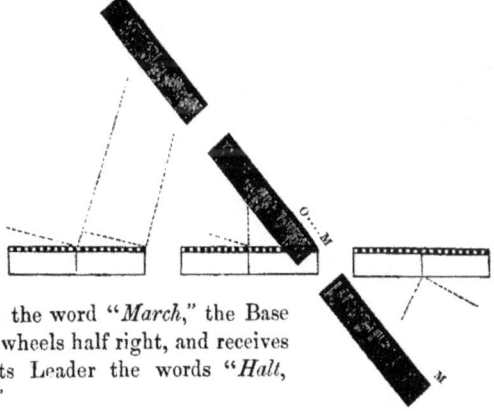

On the word *"March,"* the Base Troop wheels half right, and receives from its Leader the words *"Halt, Dress."*

The Troops on the right of the Base wheel quarter right, and receiving from the Squadron Leaders the word *"Forward,"* retire in echellon towards the new line. Each, on approaching its place, receives from its Leader the word *"Right,"* followed by *"Forward,"* and, when it has passed the line one horse's length, *"Halt, Front, Dress up."*

The Troop next on the left of the Base advances till its right uncovers the left of the Base Troop; it then receives from its Leader the word *"Right,"* followed by *"Forward, Halt, Dress up."*

---

* The Base is given by the Right Troop Leader and the Marker of the Second Squadron.

The other Troops on the left of the Base wheel quarter right, and receiving from the Squadron Leaders the word "*Forward*," advance in echellon towards the new line. Each, on approaching it, receives from its Leader the word "*Right*," followed by "*Forward*," and when on a line with the rear rank of the preceding Troop, "*Halt, Dress up.*"

Movement No. VI. from Line.

Commanding Officer, repeated by Squadron Leaders, "*Change front to the right, on the Second Squadron*.*"

Leader of the Base Troop, "*Right Troop, Right Wheel.*"

Leader of the First Squadron, "*Threes about,*" followed by "*Troops Half Right,*" as soon as the Threes have gone about.

Leader of the Troop next the Base, "*Half Right.*"

Leader of the Third Squadron, "*Troops Half Right.*"

Commanding Officer, repeated by Squadron Leaders, { "*Walk,*" or "*Trot,*" } "*March.*"

On the word "*March*," the Base Troop wheels to the right, and receives from its Leader the words "*Halt, Dress.*"

The other Troops wheel half right, and proceed to form on the new line, as directed in Movement No. V.

---

* The Base is given by the Right Troop Leader and the Marker of the Second Squadron.

MOVEMENTS FROM LINE.

OBSERVATIONS.

1. If a Change of Front is required of a less degree than in Movement No. I., it is to be done as follows:

The Commanding Officer causes the Right or Left Troop Leader of whatever Squadron he intends for the Base, to raise his sword and move forward, according to the degree of change he intends should be made. The other Troop Leader raises his sword, and puts his horse square with the intended line. Both front the Squadron. The Squadron Leader conforms by moving up to the line of his Troop Leaders, in which he is correctly placed by the Commanding Officer, or Officer appointed. The caution is then given, "*Alignment on the ——— Squadron*," which is repeated by Squadron Leaders. On the word "*March*," the named Squadron dresses up to its Officers, the other Squadrons take up the line, either by moving forward or retiring. Such as move forward are halted and dressed by their Leaders as they arrive on a line with the Base. Such as have to retire, are put Threes about upon the caution, and retiring upon the word "*March*," are again fronted, as soon as their Leaders find themselves in line with the Officers of the Base Squadron.

Movement No. VII. from Line.

Commanding Officer, repeated { *"By Threes, Change Position*
by Squadron Leaders,   *Half Right**."

"*Threes Right*"
Squadron Leaders, "~~Advance by Threes from the Right.~~"

Commanding Officer, repeated { *" Walk,* or } *March."*
by Squadron Leaders,   *" Trot,*

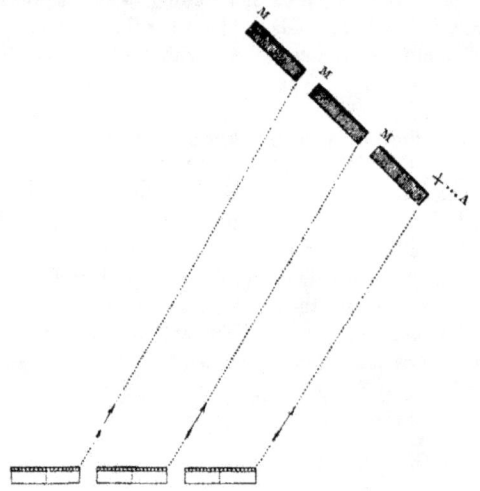

On the word "*March,*" the whole move off together.

The Squadron Leaders place themselves in front of their pivots, and conduct their Squadrons in the direction of the new Position. The Commanding Officer points out to the Leader of

---

* In Changes of Position, the Base consists of the Adjutant and Serjeant-Major, who are placed by the Major, riding out with them from the Base Squadron, when it approaches within fifty yards of the spot where the Commanding Officer intends to commence forming his line: in these movements all the Squadron Markers mark the outer points of their Squadrons.

MOVEMENTS FROM LINE. 141

the First Squadron the point where the right is to rest, and for which he is to lead straight, and at a steady pace.

The relative interval of the heads of Squadrons from each other is preserved from the First Squadron. Each, as it successively arrives within three horses' lengths of the line, receives the word "*Front Form*" from its Leader, who dresses it from the right, and then resumes his place.

OBSERVATIONS. A Change of Position, "to the Right," is made on the same principle.

This and the following movement by Threes is applicable where the ground is broken or intersected, and where the new Position will outflank the old one.

Where the nature of the ground will permit, Changes of Position of the Regiment should often be executed by the oblique echellon march of Troops. The Base Troop moves off its ground, and advances the same as the others until the line is ordered to be formed upon it*, when it wheels to complete the degree of change directed. For this purpose, the words of command will be, "*By Echellon of Troops—Change Position Half Right—to the Right—Half Right Back—or Right Back.*"

---

* The Base is placed in the same way as in the other modes of changing Position.

Movement No. VIII. from Line.

Commanding Officer, repeated by Squadron Leaders, { "*By Threes, Change Position, Half Right, Back*.*" }

Squadron Leaders, { "*Threes Left,*" ~~followed by~~ "*~~Leading Threes Half Left~~.*" }

Commanding Officer, repeated by Squadron Leaders, { "*Walk*, or "*Trot*, } *March*."

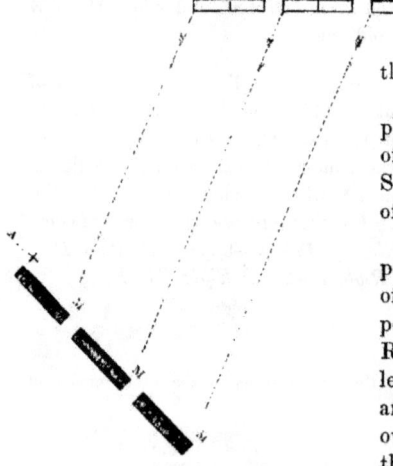

On the word "*March*," the whole move off together.

The Squadron Leaders, placing themselves in front of their pivots, conduct the Squadrons in the direction of the new Position.

The Commanding Officer points out to the Leader of the Third Squadron the point where the left of the Regiment is to rest, and he leads accordingly so as to arrive where the right of his own Squadron will stand in the line.

The relative interval of the heads of Squadrons from each other is preserved from the Third Squadron. As each Squadron successively arrives where its right is to stand in line, the Leader gives the word "*Right Wheel*" to the leading Threes, and when the head of his Squadron arrives at the point of formation, he gives the words "*Halt, Front, Dress*," from thence, and resumes his place in front of the Centre.

---

* The **Base** is placed in the same manner as in the preceding Movement.

Movement No. IX. from Line*.

Commanding Officer, repeated } "~~Open~~ *Column of Troops to*
by Squadron Leaders,   }   *the Right.*"

Leaders of Squadrons,   "*Troops Right Wheel.*"

Commanding Officer, repeated { "*Walk*, or } *March.*"
by Squadron Leaders,   { "*Trot*,   }

On the word "*March*," the Troops wheel to the right, and receive from the Squadron Leaders the words "*Halt, Dress*" (see fig. 1).

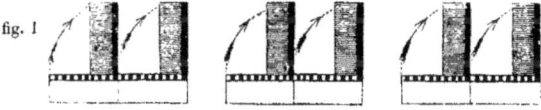

fig. 1

OBSERVATION. If the Column is wanted for immediate movement, the first part of the caution is omitted, the Commanding Officer giving merely the word "*Troops Right Wheel,*" repeated by Squadron Leaders, to whom the omission is a sign that, instead of "*Halt, Dress,*" they are to give the word "*Forward,*" at the completion of the wheel.

---

* When the Squadrons amount to 48 Files, this Movement may be executed by Divisions.

Movement No. X. from Line*.

Commanding Officer, repeated by Squadron Leaders, — "*Advance in ~~Open~~ Column from the Right.*"
Leader of the Right Troop, — "*Advance.*"
Leader of the Left Troop of the First Squadron, — "*Left Troop, Right Wheel.*"
Leaders of the Second and Third Squadrons, — "*Troops Right Wheel.*"
Commanding Officer, repeated by Squadron Leaders, — "*Walk,* or *Trot, March.*"

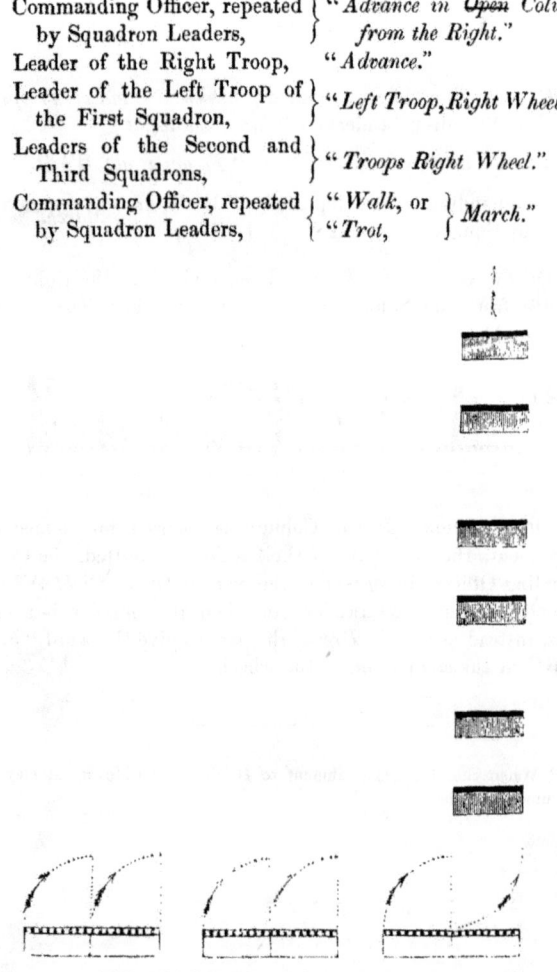

* When the Squadrons amount to 48 Files, this Movement may be executed by Divisions.

MOVEMENTS FROM LINE.

On the word "*March*," the Right Troop advances; the Troop next the leading one having completed its wheel, receives the word "*Left Wheel*," followed by "*Forward;*" the others wheel to the right, and receive the word "*Forward*" from the Squadron Leaders. Each, on reaching the wheeling point, receives from its Leader the word "*Left Wheel*," followed by "*Forward*," and follows the head of the Column.

OBSERVATION. The same movement may be done to the rear, substituting "*Retire*" for "*Advance*" in the caution, and by the Right Troop wheeling right about, and the others wheeling to the right, upon the word "*March*." But to preserve correct distances, the leading Troop should not move at its full rate of pace for the first twenty yards.

Movement No. XI. from Line*.

Commanding Officer, repeated by Squadron Leaders, { "*Column of Troops from the Right in succession by the Rear.*"

Leader of the Right Troop of the First Squadron, { "*Right Troop, Right about Wheel.*"

Commanding Officer, repeated by Squadron Leaders, { "*Walk*, or "*Trot*, } *March.*"

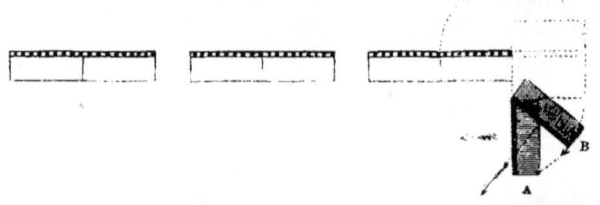

On the word "*March*," the Right Troop of the First Squadron wheels about, receives the word "*Forward*" from its Leader, moves sufficiently to the rear to clear the Serrefiles, then wheels into the "intended direction" to the right, by word from its Leader, and again receiving the word "*Forward*," continues its march.

The other Troops are, in succession, wheeled to the right-about by their Leaders, and, moving to the rear in like manner, follow in Column. Officers must take care to wheel in good time to avoid loss of interval.

The "intended direction" of the Column may either be parallel to the Line (fig. A), or oblique to it (fig. B), according as the Defile or Position, towards which the Retreat is to be made, happens to be situated.

---

* When the Squadrons amount to 48 Files, this Movement may be executed by Divisions.

Movement No. XII. from Line*.

Commanding Officer, repeated by Squadron Leaders, { "*Advance in Double Column. Right* (or *Left*) *directs.*"

Leader of the Second Squadron, "*Second Squadron Advance.*"

Leader of the First Squadron, "*Troops Left Wheel.*"

Leader of the Third Squadron, "*Troops Right Wheel.*"

Commanding Officer, repeated by Squadron Leaders, { "*Walk*, or "*Trot.* } *March.*"

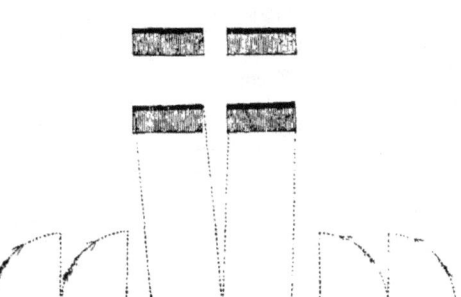

The Column of Direction is led by its Pivot: the other is led by its inward flank, and takes an interval of two horses' lengths, by inclining outwards when put in motion, which

---

* When the Squadrons amount to 48 Files, this Movement may be executed by Divisions.

interval is indispensable to the correctness of the Movement and subsequent Formation, especially when oblique to the original front.

On the word "*March*," the two centre Troops advance; the others, wheeling to the left and right, receive the word "*Forward*" from Squadron Leaders. On reaching their wheeling points, those of the right wing receive the word "*Right Wheel;*" those of the left wing, the word "*Left Wheel*" followed by "*Forward*," and follow the leading Troops in column.

Movement No. XIII. from Line.

Commanding Officer, repeated by Squadron Leaders, } "*Form Double Column on the of the Centre.*"

Leader of the Right Troop of the Second Squadron, } "*Right Troop, Advance.*"

Leader of the Left Troop of the Second Squadron, } "*Left Troop, Left Incline.*"

Leader of First Squadron, "*Threes Left.*"

Leader of Third Squadron, "*Threes Right.*"

Commanding Officer, repeated by Squadron Leaders, { "*Walk,* or "*Trot,* } *March.*"

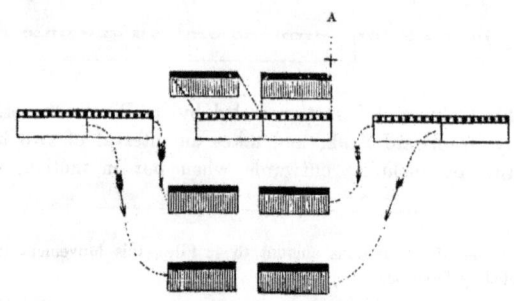

On the word "*March*," the Right Troop advances, by its right, three horses' lengths, and receives the word "*Halt, Dress*," from its Leader. The Left Troop inclines to its left, and as it gains its interval, receives the word "*Forward*," from its Leader, followed by "*Halt, Dress up*," as it comes into line with the Right Troop.

The First Squadron wheeling "Threes Left," and the Third Squadron "Threes Right," each Troop Leader goes to the pivot flank of his leading Threes, and conducts his Troop into Column; when within a few yards of the line of covering, he rides forward, and halting himself where his flank will cover, allows his Troop to pass him, and then giving the words "*Halt, Front Dress*," takes his post in front. When the Column is formed, the Right Column is usually named for direction, and dresses to its Pivot; the other to its inward flank*.

OBSERVATIONS.

1. When a Regiment is composed of four Squadrons, the heads of the Double Column are formed from the Right and Left Troops of the Second and Third Squadrons, the interval being preserved as before.

2. The Double Column can move to its flank or rear by the wheel or wheel about of Troops or Threes; wheeling up or fronting in the same manner.

---

* The Base for the covering of the Pivot of the Right Column is given by the Adjutant and the Regimental Marker.

Movement No. XIV. from Line.

Commanding Officer, repeated by Squadron Leaders, { "~~Open~~ Column *of Troops* in Rear of the Right*." }

Leader of the Base Troop, "*Right Troop Advance.*"

Leaders of the Second and Third Squadrons, and of the Troop next the Base, { "*Threes Right;*" ~~followed by "Leading Threes Half-Right.*~~" }

Commanding Officer, repeated by Squadron Leaders, { "*Walk*, or "*Trot*, } *March.*" }

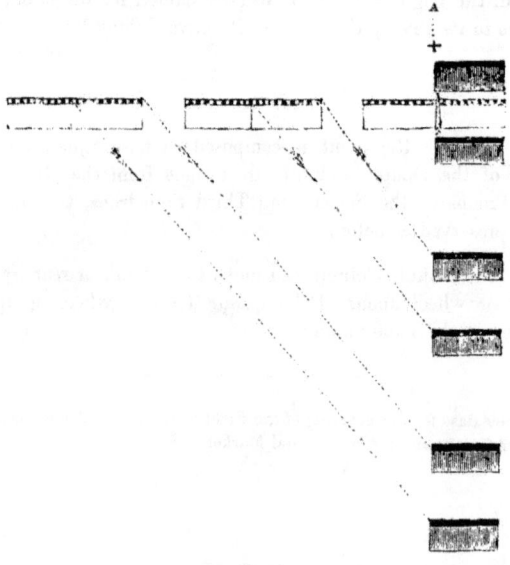

* The Base for the covering of the Pivots is given by the Adjutant and the Regimental Marker.

MOVEMENTS FROM LINE. 151

On the word "*March*," the Base Troop advances three horses' lengths, and then receives the word "*Halt, Dress*," from its Leader.

The other Troops having wheeled Threes Right, each Troop Leader places himself on the left of the leading Threes, and conducts his Troop towards its place in Column; ~~when within a few yards of the pivot line, he rides forward~~, and halting himself at the point where its left will cover, allows his Troop to pass him, and then giving the words "*Halt, Front, Dress*," takes his post in front.

OBSERVATIONS. If the Formation of an Open Column should be required in front either of Guns, or of the flank of a Line of Infantry, a Close Column must be placed or formed in front of the Guns or Flank Company, and an advance in Open Column of Troops will then give the Formation desired.

Movement No. XV. from Line.

Commanding Officer, repeated by Squadron Leaders, *"Close Column on the Second Squadron, Right in Front*."*

Leader of the First Squadron, *"First Squadron, Threes Left."*

Leader of the Third Squadron, *"Third Squadron, Threes Right."*

Commanding Officer, repeated by Squadron Leaders, *"Walk,* or *"Trot,* *March."*

On the word *"March,"*

The First Squadron having gone "Threes Left,' is conducted by its Leader (on the right flank of the leading Threes) along the front of the Second Squadron. When within a few yards of the spot where his left flank will cover, the Squadron Leader moves forward, and placing himself just beyond that point, gives the word *"Halt, Front,"* as soon as his Flank Guide will cover when wheeled up; then dresses his Squadron, and takes his post on the flank of the Column.

---

* The Base for the covering of the Pivots is given by the Regimental Marker and the Marker of the Second Squadron.

MOVEMENTS FROM LINE. 153

The Third Squadron having gone Threes Right, is conducted by its Leader (on the left flank of the leading Threes) towards its place in rear of the Second Squadron. He himself halts at the point where its left will cover on the Base, and allowing his Squadron to pass him, gives the word "*Halt, Front,*" as soon as all are past, dresses his Squadron, and then takes his post on the flank of the Column.

The above instructions are applicable to the formation of Close Column on a Flank Squadron, by naming it in the caution, and the Squadron Leaders giving their commands accordingly.

Movement No. XVII. from Line.

Commanding Officer, repeated by Squadron Leaders, { "*Inverted Line to the Rear, by the wheel about of Troops.*"

Leaders of Right Troops, "*Right Troop Advance.*"

Commanding Officer, repeated by Squadron Leaders, { "*Walk,* or "*Trot,* } *March.*"

On the word "*March,*" the Right Troop of each Squadron advances a distance equal to its front, and as soon as the Leader of the Left Troop judges he shall have room, he gives the word to his Troop, "*Right about wheel, March,*" followed by "*Halt, Dress,*" at the completion of the wheel. His word to wheel is the signal for the Leader of the Right Troop to give that Troop the word "*Left about wheel,*" followed by "*Forward,*" after the completion of the wheel, and "*Halt, Dress up,*" when on a line with the rear rank of the Left Troop (fig. 1). It must be an invariable rule that in this Movement the Right Troops advance.

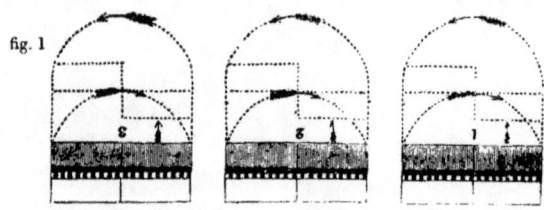

fig. 1

The Troop Leaders of the Squadron of Direction raise their swords to give a Base, as soon as that Squadron has formed.

1. If, from Inverted Line, it is desired to restore the proper order of the Squadrons, the caution will be, "*Reverse the Front by the wheel about of Troops**,*" and the Movement proceeds as already detailed above.

---

* This word of command, "*Reverse the Front by the wheel about of Troops,*" is to be used for a Squadron when acting singly.

MOVEMENTS FROM LINE.

2. Although the above is to be the usual practice, the Line may occasionally be inverted to the rear, by the Commanding Officer merely giving the word, "*Squadrons Right about,* (or *Left about,*) *Wheel,*" repeated by Squadron Leaders; and on the word "*March,*" they wheel about accordingly (see fig. 2). The proper order of Squadrons may be restored by the same method.

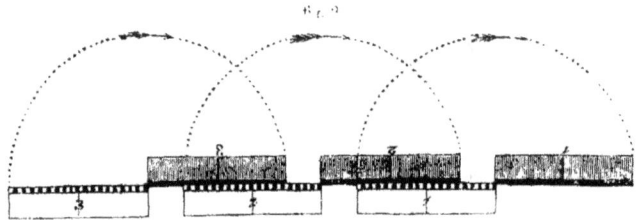

3. An Inverted Line can change its Front or Position in the same manner as if it was in its proper order. But, in the Commands, Squadrons must always be designated by their proper numbers, as First, Second, Third, &c., and not according to their situation in the Inverted Line.

4. If an Inverted Line is required to march off in Open Column to a flank, and it is desirable to restore its proper order (suppose Right in Front), the caution is, "*Column of Troops from the Right of Squadrons to the Left,*" on which the Right Troops advance three horses' lengths, wheel to the left, and move on along the front of the Left Troops, which, as soon as they have space, advance, wheel, and follow their Right Troops.

Movement No. XVIII. from Line.

DIRECT ECHELLON.

Commanding Officer, repeated by Squadron Leaders, } *"Advance in Echellon from the Right."*

Leader of the First Squadron,   *"First Squadron Advance."*

Commanding Officer, repeated by Squadron Leaders, } *"Walk,* or *"Trot,* } *March."*

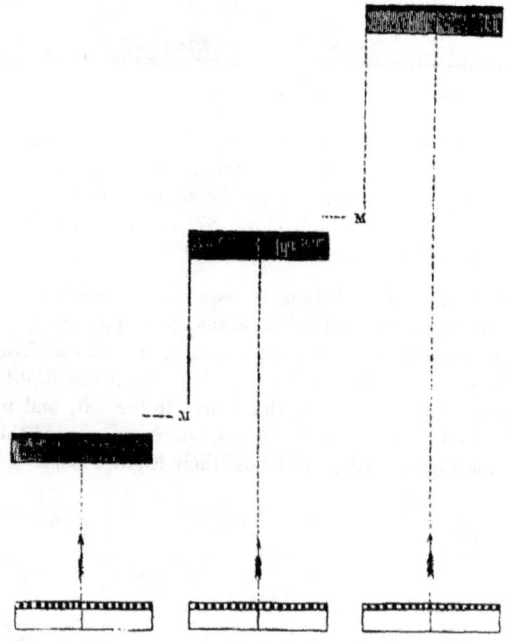

On the word *"March,"* the First Squadron advances. The remaining Squadrons receive the word *"March"* from their Leaders in succession, as soon as each has got a distance equal to its front and interval, from the preceding Squadron.

MOVEMENTS FROM LINE.

1. The Marker of each Squadron places himself at the space of a Squadron interval from the inward flank of his own Squadron, a little in advance of the line of Officers, and exactly covering the flank file of the Squadron which precedes him. In the advance he preserves his station correctly, and thus enables his own Squadron Leader to judge the proper interval from the Squadron in his front.

2. The Retreat in Echellon is exactly like the Advance, each Squadron going Threes About, in sufficient time not to lose its distance from the one before it. In the caution the word "*Retire*" is substituted for "*Advance.*"

3. Each Squadron should move at a distance equal to its Front and Interval, unless otherwise ordered.

4. When Squadrons, having advanced in Direct Echellon, are required to form line to the front, a Squadron of Formation is named, whose Troop Leaders give the Base. The Squadrons in front (if any) are put about by Threes, and the whole move into line upon the named Squadron.

5. When a Formation into Line is required to the left, the Squadrons wheel to that hand, and form line upon a named Squadron.

6. If, while advancing in Direct Echellon from the right, it is suddenly required to form an Oblique Line towards the left, the command is given "*Oblique Line to the Left,*" and the Squadrons, wheeling to that hand a sufficient degree to place them in line, receive the word "*Forward*" from their Leaders, and immediately advance by the usual Squadron of Direction, correcting their intervals from that Squadron as they move forward.

Movement No. XIX. from Line.

Commanding Officer, repeated by Squadron Leaders, { "*Retire by Alternate Squadrons.*" }

Leaders of even Numbers (Squadrons), "*Threes About.*"

Commanding Officer, repeated by Squadron Leaders, { "*Walk,* or "*Trot,* } *March.*"

On the word "*March,*" the Second Squadron (also the Fourth, if there be one,) having gone Threes About, retires about 100 yards, and receives from its Leader the word "*Halt, Front,*" upon which the First and Third Squadrons receive from their Leaders the word "*Threes About,*" and retire till they have passed the Second, the same distance as above. They then front, and the Second goes about by Threes, and so on, until the Commanding Officer orders the line to be formed on one of the Squadrons, the Troop Leaders of which raise their swords to give the Base.

1. The halting and fronting of each Line may be regulated according to the discretion of the Commanding Officer, by a Trumpet Signal; but it is an invariable rule that the Front Line does not go about until the Retiring Line has halted and fronted.

2. The Retreat of each Line must be guided by a Squadron of Direction; and either flank may be thrown back, and the direction of the Line changed, during the retreat, if required. The Major takes the temporary command of the Second Line, or even numbers.

Movement No. XIX. from Line.

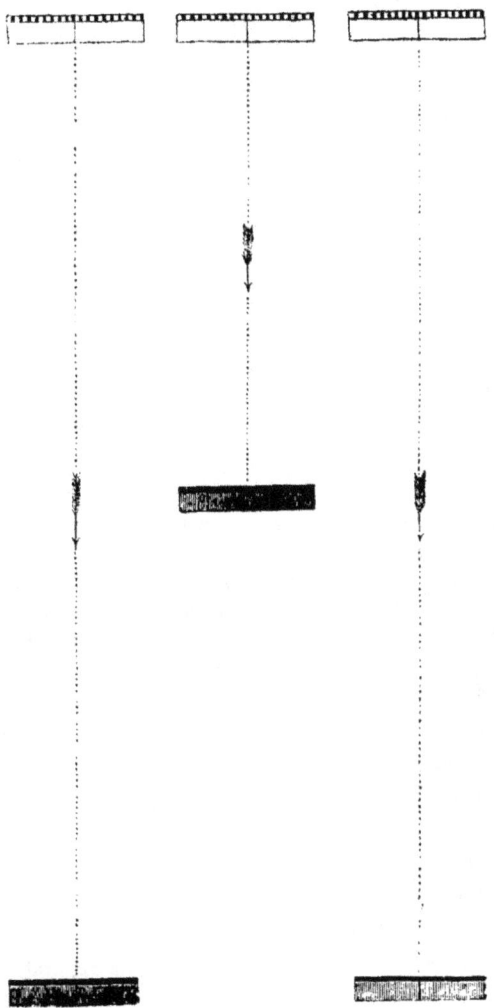

Movement No. XX. from Line.

PASSAGE OF LINES TO THE FRONT.

Commanding Officer, repeated by Squadron Leaders, { "*Advance by Threes from the Right of Squadrons.*"

Commanding Officer, repeated by Squadron Leaders, { "*Walk*, or "*Trot*, } *March.*"

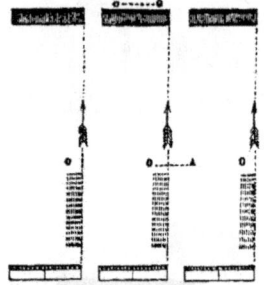

On the word "*March*," each Squadron advances in Column of Threes, through the intervals made for it by the Line in its front; when the Line is to be formed again, the Commanding Officer gives the word "*Front form*," (which is repeated by Squadron Leaders,) and each Squadron forms on its leading Threes, the Leaders dressing them from the right and then resuming their posts.

1. In this movement, Squadron Leaders are to be in front of their leading Threes.

2. A moving Base is given for the heads of Squadrons by the Leader of the Squadron of Direction and the Adjutant, who rides about twenty yards from him.

3. Either flank may be thrown forward during the advance by an alteration in the direction of the Base.

4. This and the following Movement are applicable to the passage over broken ground, as well as to the Passage of Lines, whether of Cavalry or Infantry.

Movement No. XXI. from Line.

Passage of Lines to the Rear.

Commanding Officer, repeated by Squadron Leaders, { "*Retire by Threes from the Right of Squadrons.*"

Squadron Leaders, { "*Threes Right—Leading Threes Right Wheel.*"

Commanding Officer, repeated by Squadron Leaders, { "*Walk,* or "*Trot,* } *March.*"

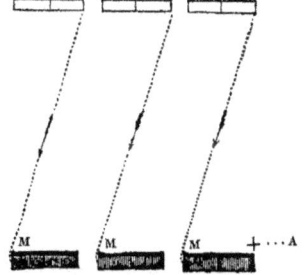

On the word "*March,*" each Squadron retires in Column of Threes. Squadron Leaders are in front of their leading Threes, and the intervals of heads of Squadrons from each other are preserved from the first Squadron. During the march of the Columns, a moving Base is given, by the Leader of the First Squadron and the Adjutant. When the Columns approach within fifty yards of the place where the Commanding Officer intends to re-form his line, the Major, or Officer appointed, rides forward, and places a fixed Base for the purpose, consisting of the Adjutant and Serjeant-Major, where the right of the first Squadron is to stand. Squadron Markers then move out and mark the left points of Squadrons, and each Leader, conducting his Squadron to its own left point, gives the word "*Leading Threes, Left Wheel, Forward,*" moves on with his Squadron, and when its head has arrived at the point of Formation, gives the word "*Halt, Front,*" and resumes his post in front of the centre.

Observation. This Movement must not be used for retiring through Infantry, unless when in Squares.

Section XII. ON THE CLOSE COLUMN.

1. The general objects of a Close Column are, to form Line to the front in the quickest manner, to conceal numbers, and to extend in whatever direction the circumstances of the moment may require. It is a situation for the Assembly rather than for the Movement of Cavalry, and is more applicable to Reserves than to the general purposes of Field Movement.

The Close Column is composed of Squadrons, except in the case of its being required to assemble in very confined situations, where it may be more desirable to form a Column of Troops, on which occasions the Leaders of Troops must move out to the pivot, and the Serrefiles to the reverse flank; but when it is moved into open ground to deploy, the Column of Squadrons will be formed, and closed to its front, before the deployment takes place.

2. The Close Column, whether of Squadrons, or Troops, dresses to the pivot flank both when halted and in movement; except when a Formation is ordered to the reverse flank. After wheeling by Threes to take ground to a flank, or for the purpose of deployment, the dressing and preservation of distances are to what was the Front of the Column.

3. When the Close Column is to take ground to a flank, the Caution is given "*Take ground to the Right or Left*," on which the Threes are wheeled to the hand ordered, and the whole move on the word "*March*," Dressing and Distance being preserved from the Squadron at the head of the Column.

4. The Close Column can change its direction on a Moveable Pivot by the command "*Right* (or *Left*) *Shoulders*" followed by "*Forward.*"

5. Should it be required to deploy into an Oblique Line, a previous command is given, "*Squadrons Quarter* (or Half) *Right*," upon which each Squadron wheels as it stands in Column upon its own right flank man, so that the Column is in Oblique Echellon. The Deployment, on any named Squadron, then proceeds in the usual way.

ON THE CLOSE COLUMN.

6. The Deployment on the front Squadron should sometimes be practised from Close Column in march to the front. On such occasions, the Deployment must be made at double the rate at which the leading body is moving.

7. When from Close Column of Squadrons, it is required to advance in Open Column of Troops, the Right Troop of the First Squadron receives from its Leader, on the Caution, the word "*Advance.*" On the word "*March,*" the Right Troop advances, and the Left Troop receives from its Leader the words "*Right Incline, March,*" followed by "*Forward,*" when it covers the preceding Troop in Column. The remaining Squadrons break into Open Column of Troops in the same manner, when it comes to their turn.

MOVEMENTS FROM CLOSE COLUMN.

Movement No. I. from Close Column.

Commanding Officer, "*Deploy on the First Squadron*.*"

Leaders of the Second and Third Squadrons, "*Threes Left.*"

Commanding Officer, { "*Walk,* or "*Trot,*" } *March.*"

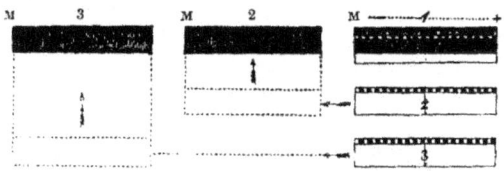

On the word "*March,*" the Leader of the First Squadron dresses it up to the Markers, and the Second and Third Squadrons lead out to the left. As soon as the former is opposite its place in line, it receives from its Leader the words "*Second Squadron, Halt, Front, Forward,*" and when on a line with the rear rank of the First Squadron, "*Halt, Dress up.*"

In like manner, when the Third Squadron arrives opposite its place, it receives the words "*Third Squadron, Halt, Front, Forward,*" and when on a line with the rear rank of the Second Squadron, "*Halt, Dress up.*"

---

* On the caution to deploy, the Base is given by the Regimental Marker, and the Marker of the First Squadron, who are placed one horse's length in advance of the head of the Column. The Marker of the Second Squadron also takes his post at the caution.

Movement No. II. from Close Column.

Commanding Officer, "*Deploy on the Third Squadron**."

Leaders of the First and Second Squadrons, "*Threes Right.*"

Commanding Officer, { "*Walk*, or "*Trot*, } March."

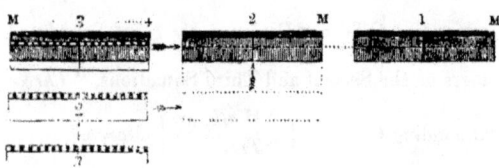

On the word "*March*," the First and Second Squadrons lead out to the right; the latter, when opposite its place in the line, receives from its Leader the words "*Second Squadron, Halt, Front*," followed by "*Forward*," as soon as its front is clear, and when on a line with the rear rank of the Third Squadron, "*Halt, Dress up*." The First Squadron has only to march straight along the Alignment, and receives from its Leader the words "*First Squadron, Halt, Front, Dress*," when it reaches its place.

The Third Squadron, the moment its front is clear, receives from its Leader the word "*March*," and when it has moved up to the Markers, "*Halt, Dress*."

Central Deployment.

The Deployment upon the Second (Central) Squadron is equally necessary as upon the Head or Rear, and should be as often practised.

The First Squadron wheels "Threes Right," and proceeds as in Deployment upon the Rear Squadron; the Third wheels

---

* On the caution to deploy, the Base is given by the Regimental Marker, and the Marker of the Third Squadron, who are placed one horse's length in advance of the head of the Column. The Marker of the Second Squadron also takes his post on the caution.

CLOSE COLUMN.

"Threes Left," and proceeds as in Deployment upon the Head Squadron; while the Second, as soon as its front is clear, moves

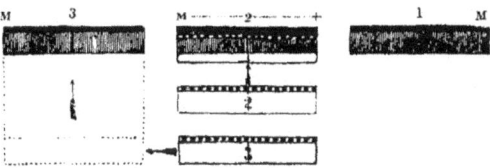

up to the Base marked for it upon the Alignment. On the caution to Deploy, the Base is given by the Regimental Marker and the Marker of the Second Squadron, one horse's length in advance of the head of the Column. The Markers of the First and Third Squadrons also take post on the caution.

OBLIQUE DEPLOYMENT.

Should it be required to Deploy into an Oblique Line, the previous command will be given, "*Squadrons, Quarter (or Half) Right,*" or "*Quarter (or Half) Left,*" upon which each Squadron wheels the degree ordered, so that the Column stands in Oblique Echellon, the Head Squadron being thus placed on the intended Alignment. The Deployment then proceeds in the usual way.

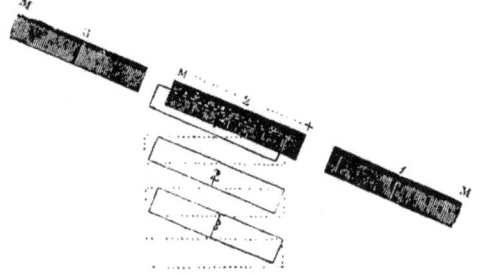

If, on a Rear or Central Squadron, the Base must, of course, be placed at the points where the flanks of that Squadron will arrive when it shall have moved up to the Alignment, without regard to the flanks of the Head Squadron. Officers turn their own horses upon the caution, in the same direction as the Squadron to which they respectively belong will march, when the Deployment begins.

Movement No. III. from Close Column.

Commanding Officer, { "*Form Line to the Left on the Third Squadron*.*" }

Leader of the Third Squadron, "*Third Squadron Left Wheel.*"
Leaders of the First and Second Squadrons, "*Advance.*"

Commanding Officer, { "*Walk,* or "*Trot,* } March."

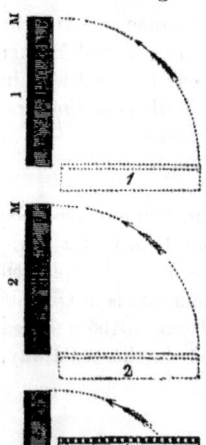

On the word "*March,*" the First and Second Squadrons advance; each, as soon as it has got proper distance, receiving from its Leader the word "*Left Wheel,*" followed by "*Forward,*" and "*Halt, Dress,*" as it comes up to the line of the Third Squadron; each Leader being on the left flank of the Column to halt his Squadron.

The Third Squadron wheels to the Left, and receives from its Leader the word "*Forward,*" followed by "*Halt, Dress up,*" when it has moved up three horses' lengths.

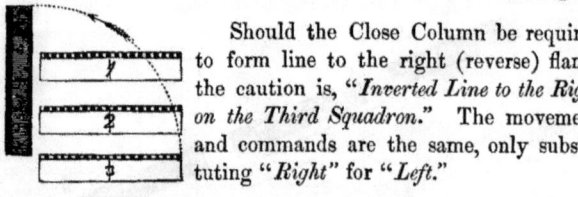

Should the Close Column be required to form line to the right (reverse) flank, the caution is, "*Inverted Line to the Right on the Third Squadron.*" The movement and commands are the same, only substituting "*Right*" for "*Left.*"

OBSERVATIONS. To form the Line on the First Squadron, the Second and Third are put about by Threes, moved to the rear till they have got their proper distances, and then halted, fronted, and wheeled into line. To form the Line on the Second Squadron, the Third is put about and moved back, and the First moved forward, on the same principle.

---

* On the caution, the Base is given by the Marker of the Third Squadron, posted opposite its left flank, and the Regimental Marker posted twelve *yards* on his right hand.

Movement No. IV. from Close Column.

"*Change Front to the Right*.*"

Leader of the First Squadron, { "*First Squadron Right Wheel.*" }

Leaders of the Second and Third Squadrons, "*Threes Left.*"

Commanding Officer, { "*Walk,* or "*Trot,* } *March.*"

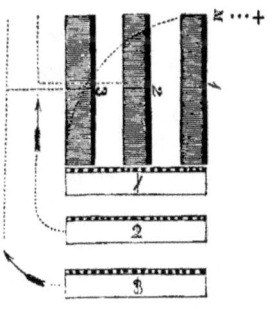

On the word "*March,*" the First Squadron wheels to the right, and receives from its Leader the word "*Halt, Dress.*" The Leaders of the Second and Third Squadrons conduct them circling into the new direction. They halt, and front them in succession as they cover, and moving them up by the word "*Forward,*" give the word "*Halt, Dress,*" as each gains its proper distance from the front.

---

* On the caution, the Base for the covering of the Pivots is given by the Regimental Marker and the Marker of the First Squadron.

Movement No. V. from Close Column.

Commanding Officer, "*The Column will reverse its Front*.*"

Leaders of Right Troops, "*Right Troop, Threes about.*"

Commanding Officer, { "*Walk*, or "*Trot*, } *March.*"

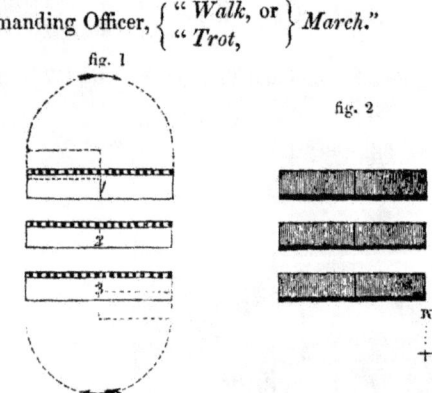

On the word "*March*," both Columns of Troops advance two horses' lengths; the Commanding Officer then gives the words, "*Leading Troops, Right about Wheel,*" and "*Forward,*" when the wheel is completed; the rest follow, and wheel on the same ground, receiving the words from their Troop Leaders, until the Right and Left Troops of the Column have completely changed places (fig. 1). The Commanding Officer then gives the word "*Halt, Front,*" on which the whole halt, and the Right Troops front (fig. 2). Squadron Leaders dress their Squadrons from the pivot flanks, and then resume their usual posts.

It is a rule for the ~~Right~~ Troops always to go about by Threes in this Movement, whether the Right or Left be in front, and they will be led by their ~~inward~~ flanks.

---

* On the caution, the Base for the covering of the Pivot is given by the Regimental Marker and the Marker of the First Squadron.

Movement No. VI. from Close Column.

Commanding Officer, "*The Squadrons will Countermarch**."

Squadron Leaders, "*Threes Right and Left.*"

Commanding Officer, { "*Walk,* or "*Trot,* } "*March.*"

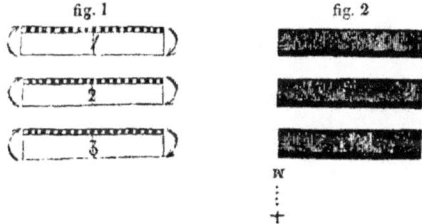

On the word "*March,*" the leading Three of each rank, advancing half a horse's length, wheels "right about" on its right-hand man, the rest following and wheeling at the same point, till the front and rear ranks have exactly changed places (fig. 1). The Squadron Leaders, remaining on the pivot flank, give the words "*Halt, Front, Dress*" (fig. 2); and, having dressed the ranks, resume their places.

During the Countermarch, the Troop Leaders move on the flank of their leading Threes of the front rank.

Whether the Column be right or left in front, it is to be a rule that the front rank always goes Threes Right, and the rear rank Threes Left.

---

* On the caution, the Base for the covering of the Pivots is given by the Regimental Marker and the Marker of the Third Squadron.

173

SECTION XIII. ON THE OPEN COLUMN.

1. MOVEMENTS of the Open Column to front, rear, and flanks, are of the utmost importance, and, as they precede many Formations into Line, the greatest attention should be paid to their exactness. The Open Column is called "Column of Route," when applied to common Marches. It is named the "Column of Manœuvre," when applied to the execution of Field Movements, and the greatest precision is then required, in order to ensure at any moment a correct Formation into Line. The Column will be formed with the left in front, whenever it is probable that the Formation of the Line will be required to the right flank, and right in front when required to the left.

2. The Open Column of Troops is to be considered the established Column of Manœuvre.

3. It is a general rule, that, in all Formations of Line from Open Column by the Oblique Echellon, the Troops must rather over-wheel at the commencement of the Movement; those next the Base making nearly a full wheel.

4. In the following Movements from Open Column, no Formations of Line oblique to the direction of the Column have been laid down, it being considered the safest for the Column previously to form Line in the prolongation of its front, or either of its flanks; having done this, it is easy for the Line immediately to make such a change of Front as may place it in the required situation.

5. When the Open Column is to take ground to its flank, the caution is given "*Take Ground to the Right* (or *Left*)," on which the Threes are wheeled, and the Troop Leaders place themselves in front of the pivot flank of their leading Threes. During the movement they preserve their dressing and distances from the head of the Column, from whence a Base is given by the Adjutant and the Leader of the Troop at the head of the Column.

6. The Head of an Open Column can change direction on a Moveable Pivot by the commands "*Head of the Column*," "*Left*

Shoulders," followed by "*Forward;*" or when a precise degree of change is intended, the words may be given "*Head of the Column,*" "*Quarter Right,*" or "*Half Right,*" or "*Right Wheel,*" followed by "*Forward.*"

7. The Open Column can change front to the extent of the quarter-circle on the head Troop of the Leading Squadron; that Troop being placed in the required direction, all the other Troops wheel by Threes to the pivot or reverse flank, and proceed to form in Column in the new direction. This Movement, of changing front on the head Troop of an Open Column, may be required when taking up ground with other Regiments. The head of the Column being led to where it is to stand, and the leading Troop wheeled into the intended direction, the Caution is given, "*Enter the new Direction to the Right* (or *Left*)," and the whole, by flank marching, form in rear of the leading Troop.

8. The Open Column can retire either by "Threes about," or by the Troops "Wheeling about," or "Countermarching."

9. Double Column Movements are very useful for taking up oblique Positions; for the passage of Defiles of a sufficient width, where no impediment is likely to occur in the subsequent Formation of the Line; but where obstacles and narrow passes are to be expected, the single Column is less liable to confusion, and is, therefore, better adapted for general circumstances. For the Formation and Movements of Supports and Reserves in Brigade, Double Columns are both safe and convenient.

MOVEMENTS FROM OPEN COLUMN.

Movement No. I. from Open Column.

Commanding Officer, repeated by Squadron Leaders, { "*Left Wheel into Line**." "*Walk*, or "*Trot*, } *March.*"

On the caution, the Leaders of the Second and Third Squadrons face the pivot line at the point where the centres of their Squadron will rest, dressing upon the Base.

On the word "*March*," the Troops wheel left into line, receiving the word "*Halt, Dress*," from the Squadron Leaders, as they complete the wheel. The Troop Leaders, during the wheel, will place themselves in the line of dressing, fronting the centres of their Troops. The Standard and his Coverer resume their posts in Squadron during the wheel. At the completion of the wheel the word is given "*Eyes Front*," repeated by Squadron Leaders, upon which the Officers and Markers resume their places.

OBS. 1. When a Column of Divisions wheels into line, the Base is given in like manner; the Troop Leaders placing themselves in the line of dressing opposite the pivot file of their Leading Divisions.

2. Wheeling into Line without halting is a most necessary practice for Service. The caution is the same as when halted, and is repeated by Squadron Leaders. At the completion of the wheels, Squadron Leaders give the word "*Forward*," and the Line advances at the former pace. All the Officers take their dressing from the Squadron of Direction. No Markers are employed, nor do Troop Leaders front their Troops during the wheel.

---

* The Base is given by the Marker and Right Troop Leader of the First Squadron.

Movement No. II. from Open Column.

Commanding Officer, repeated } "*Form Line to the Front*.*"
by Squadron Leaders,

Leader of the Base Troop, "*Right Troop Advance.*"

Leader of the Troop next the Base, "*Left Troop Half Left.*"

~~Squadron Leaders,~~ "*Troops Half Left.*"

Commanding Officer, repeated { "*Walk,* or } "*March.*"
by Squadron Leaders, { "*Trot,*

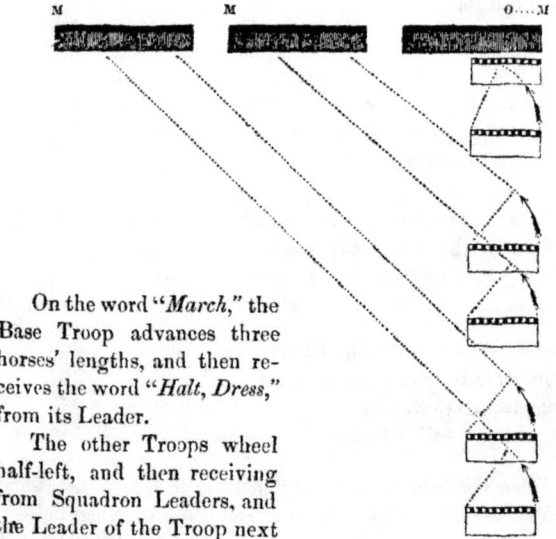

On the word "*March,*" the Base Troop advances three horses' lengths, and then receives the word "*Halt, Dress,*" from its Leader.

The other Troops wheel half-left, and then receiving from Squadron Leaders, and the Leader of the Troop next the Base, the word "*Forward,*" advance in Echellon towards their point in the Line. Each, as it approaches, receives from its Leader the word "*Right,*" followed by "*Forward;*" and, on arriving on a line with the rear rank of the preceding Troop, "*Halt, Dress up.*"

---

* The Base is given by the Marker and Right Troop Leader of the First Squadron.

Movement No. III. from Open Column.

Commanding Officer, repeated by Squadron Leaders, { "*Form Line to the Front on the Rear Troop*.*" }

Leader of the Troop next the Base, "*Right Troop Half Left.*"

~~Squadron Leaders~~, "*Troops Half Left.*"

Commanding Officer, repeated by Squadron Leaders, { "*Walk*, or "*Trot*, } *March.*"

On the word "*March*," the whole, except the Base Troop (which stands fast), move as follows:

The Troops wheel half-left, and receiving the words "*Halt*," "*Threes about*," followed by "*Forward*," from Squadron Leaders and the Leader of the Troop next the Base, retire in Echellon towards their places in the Line. Each, on approaching the Line, receives from its Leader the word "*Right*," followed by "*Forward*," and, when it has passed the Line one horse's length, "*Halt, Front, Dress up.*"

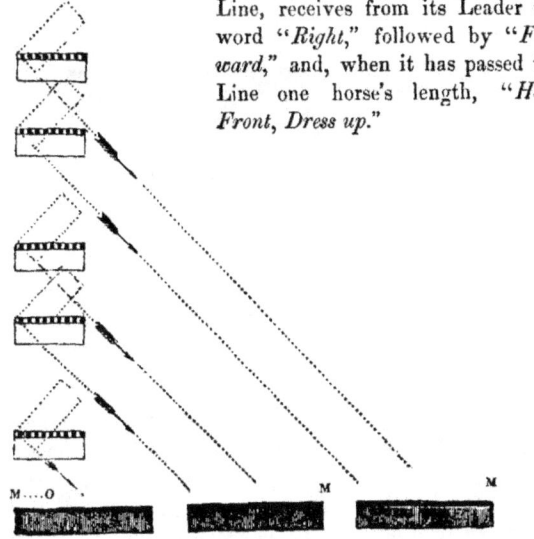

---

* The Base is given by the Marker and Left Troop Leader of the Third Squadron.

Movement No. IV. from Open Column.

Commanding Officer, repeated by Squadron Leaders, *"Form Line to the Front on the Second Squadron*."*

Leader of the Base Troop, *"Right Troop Advance."*

Leader of the Troop in rear of the Base. *"Left Troop Half Left."*

~~Squadron Leaders,~~ *"Troops Half Left."*

Commanding Officer, repeated by Squadron Leaders, *"Walk,* or *"Trot,* } *March."*

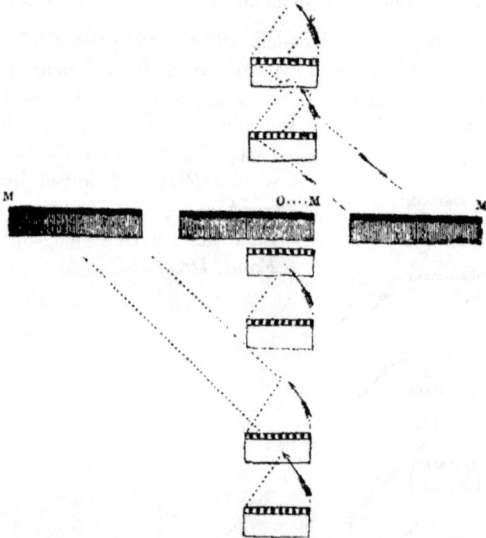

On the word *"March,"* the Base Troop advances three horses' lengths, and then receives the word *"Halt, Dress,"* from its Leader.

The other Troops wheel half left, those in front of the Base going "Threes about" as soon as the wheel is completed; and the formation then proceeds as in Movements Nos. II. and III.

---

* The Base is given by the Marker and Right Troop Leader of the Second Squadron.

Movement No. V. from Open Column.

Commanding Officer, repeated by Squadron Leaders, } "*Form Line to the Rear on the Leading Troop*.*"

Leader of the Base Troop, "*Right Troop Left about Wheel.*"

Leaders of Squadrons and Troop next the Base, } "*Threes Right.*"

Commanding Officer, repeated by Squadron Leaders, { "*Walk*, or "*Trot*, } *March.*"

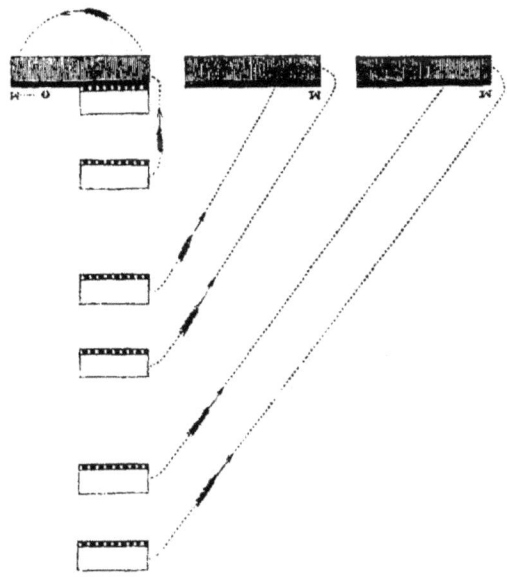

On the word "*March*," the Base Troop wheels Left about, and receives the word "*Halt, Dress*," from its Leader.

---

* The Base is given by the Marker and Right Troop Leader of the First Squadron.

MOVEMENTS FROM OPEN COLUMN.

The other Troops ~~move off together, and~~ are conducted by their Leaders (on the left flank of the leading Threes) to the points where their Left will stand in the new line, that for the inward Troop being marked by the Squadron Leader, and that for the outward by the Squadron Marker. ~~Each Troop Leader then gives the words "*Leading Threes Left Wheel,*" followed by "*Forward,*" and "*Halt, Front, Dress,*" when the whole have passed round, and the head of the Troop has arrived at its point of formation; he then takes his post.~~

Movement No. VI. from Open Column.

Commanding Officer, repeated by Squadron Leaders, { "*Form Line to the Rear on the Rear Troop*.*" }

Leader of the Base Troop, "*Left Troop Left about Wheel.*"

Leaders of Squadrons and Troops next the Base, { "*Troops Three Quarters Left about.*" }

Commanding Officer, repeated by Squadron Leaders, { "*Walk*, or "*Trot*, } *March.*"

On the word "*March*," the Base Troop wheels "*Left about*," receives from its Leader the word "*Forward*," and, advancing three horses' lengths, "*Halt, Dress.*" The other Troops wheel three-quarters left about, and, receiving the word "*Forward*" from Squadron Leaders, and Leader of the Troop next the Base, advance in Echellon towards their places in the Line.

Each, on approaching it, receives from its Leader the word "*Left*," followed by "*Forward;*" and, on arriving on a line with the rear rank of the preceding Troop, "*Halt, Dress up.*"

---

* The Base is given by the Marker and Left Troop Leader of the Third Squadron.

Movement No. VII. from Open Column.

Commanding Officer, repeated by Squadron Leaders, { "*Form Line to the Rear on the Second Squadron*.*" }

Leader of the Base Troop, "*Left Troop Left about Wheel.*"

Leaders of Squadrons, and of the Troop before the Base, { "*Troops Three Quarters Left about.*" }

Leaders of Squadrons behind the Base, "*Threes Right.*"

Commanding Officer, repeated by Squadron Leaders, { "*Walk*, or "*Trot*, } March."

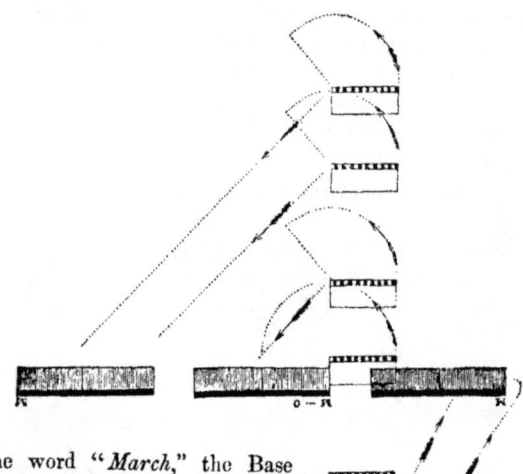

On the word "*March*," the Base Troop wheels left about, receives from its Leader the word "*Forward*," and, advancing three horses' lengths, "*Halt, Dress.*" The Troops before the Base wheel three-quarters left about, and form as prescribed in Movement No. VI. The Troops in rear of the Base move off together, and form as laid down in Movement No. V.

---

* The Base is given by the Marker and Left Troop Leader of the Second Squadron.

Movement No. VIII. from Open Column.

A Column having changed its direction to the reverse (right) hand forms line to its former front, as follows:

Commanding Officer, repeated by Squadron Leaders, } *"Form Line to the Left on the new Alignment*."*

Leaders of the First and Second Squadrons, } *"Left Wheel into Line."*

Leader of the Right Troop of the Third Squadron, } *"Right Troop Advance."*

Leader of the Left Troop of the Third Squadron, } *"Left Troop Half Left."*

Commanding Officer, repeated by Squadron Leaders, } { *"Walk,* or *"Trot,* } *March."*

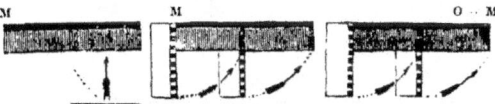

On the word *"March,"* the Troops of the First and Second Squadrons, wheeling left into Line, receive the word *"Halt, Dress,"* from Squadron Leaders. The Right Troop of the Third Squadron advances till on a line with the rear rank of the Second Squadron, and then receives, from its Leader, the word *"Halt, Dress up."* The Left Troop of the Third Squadron, wheeling half-left, receives from its Leader the word *"Forward,"* then, on approaching the Line, *"Right,"* followed by *"Forward,"* and, when it arrives on a line with the rear rank of the preceding Troop, *"Halt, Dress up."*

Should the new Line be oblique to the old one, instead of at right angles with it, the degree of wheel for the rear of the Column will depend on the change of direction its head has made. In this case the leading Troop of that part of the Column which is yet in the old direction will be placed on the new Alignment, according to the degree of its obliquity.

---

* The Base is given by the Marker and Right Troop Leader of the First Squadron.

Movement No. IX. from Open Column.

A Column having changed its direction to the pivot (left) hand, forms line to its former rear, as follows:

Commanding Officer, repeated by Squadron Leaders, *"Form Line to the Left on the new Alignment*."*

Leaders of the First and Second Squadrons, *"Left Wheel into Line."*

Leader of the Third Squadron, *"Threes Right."*

Commanding Officer, repeated by Squadron Leaders, *"Walk,* or *"Trot, March."*

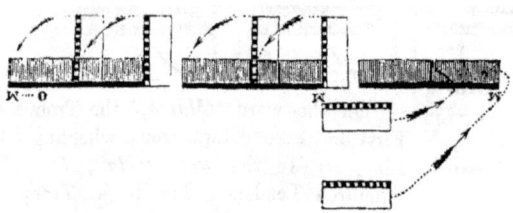

On the word *"March,"* the Troops of the First and Second Squadrons wheel into Line, as detailed in Movement No. I.

The Troops of the Third Squadron move off together, and form as detailed in Movement No. V. from Open Column.

OBSERVATIONS. The change of direction of a Column, followed by this or the preceding Movement, is a convenient method for forming a Regiment across the Road on which it was marching, or for covering the entrance or issue of a Defile.

---

* The Base is given by the Marker and Right Troop Leader of the First Squadron.

Movement No. X. from Open Column.

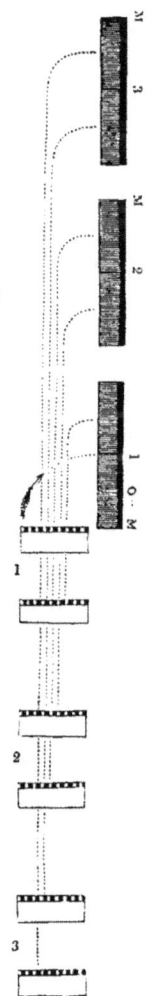

Commanding Officer, repeated by Squadron Leaders, } *"To the Reverse Flank, Right form Line*."*

Leader of the Base Troop, } *"Right Troop Right Wheel."*

Commanding Officer, repeated by Squadron Leaders, } *"Walk,* or *"Trot,* } *March."*

On the word *"March,"* the leading Troop wheels to the right, receives the word *"Forward"* from its Leader, and, when it has advanced three horses' lengths, *"Halt, Dress."*

The other Troops pass along the rear of the leading Troop; each in succession, as soon as its flank comes opposite its place in the Line, receives from its Leader the words *"Right Wheel—Forward;"* and, when on a line with the rear rank of the preceding Troop, *"Halt, Dress up."*

---

* The Base is given by the Marker and Right Troop Leader of the First Squadron.

Movement No. XI. from Open Column.

Commanding Officer, repeated by Squadron Leaders, { "*Form Inverted Line to the Right, on the Heads of Squadrons*.*" }

Leaders of Right Troops, "*Right Troop Right Wheel.*"

Leaders of Left Troops, "*Left Troop Advance.*"

Commanding Officer, repeated by Squadron Leaders, { "*Walk,* or "*Trot,* } *March.*"

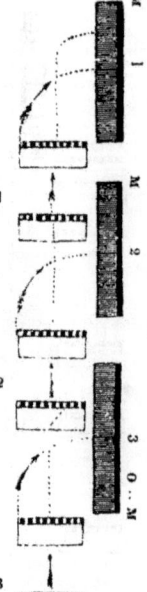

On the word "*March,*" the Right Troops wheel to the right, receive from their Leaders the word "*Forward,*" and then, advancing four horses' lengths, "*Halt, Dress.*"

The Left Troops pass along the rear of the Right Troops of their own Squadrons; when clear of their left flanks, receive the word "*Right wheel,*" followed by "*Forward;*" and, when on a line with the rear rank of the other Troops, "*Halt, Dress up.*"

---

* The Base is given by the Marker and Right Troop Leader of the Third Squadron.

Movement No. XII. from Open Column.

Commanding Officer, repeated by Squadron Leaders, } "*Form Inverted Line to the Front*.*"

Leader of the Base Troop, "*Right Troop Advance.*"

Leader of the Left Troop of the First Squadron, } "*Left Troop, Half Left.*"

Leaders of Right Troops of Second and Third Squadrons, } "*Right Troop, Right Wheel.*"

Commanding Officer, repeated by Squadron Leaders, } { "*Walk,* or "*Trot,* } *March.*"

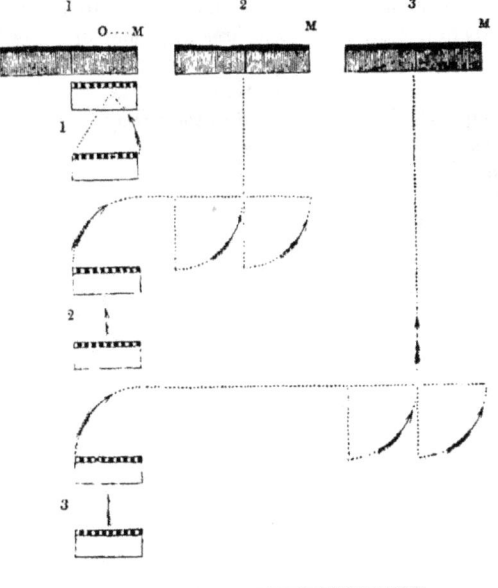

---

* The Base is given by the Right Troop Leader of the First Squadron, and the Marker of that Squadron, placed opposite its right flank.

MOVEMENTS FROM OPEN COLUMN.

On the word "*March*," the Leading Troop of the First Squadron advances three horses' lengths, and then receives the word "*Halt, Dress*," from its Leader. The Left Troop of that Squadron forms on the Right Troop, as in Movement No. II.

The Right Troops of the Second and Third Squadrons wheel to the right, and receive from their Leaders the word "*Forward:*" their Left Troops advance, and, wheeling at the same point, follow in column; and, when the left flank of the latter has nearly gained the Squadron Interval, the Squadron Leader gives the word "*Left Wheel into Line,*" and "*Forward,*" at the completion of the wheel. Each Squadron is then led by its centre, and, on coming in line with the rear rank of the Base Squadron, receives the word "*Halt, Dress up.*"

OBSERVATION. The object of this Movement is to enable an Open Column, arriving, with its right in front, at a place where there is want of space or broken ground upon its left, to form line instantly to the front without the delay of changing the direction of the head of the Column to the right, and then marching with the flank exposed to the enemy, before wheeling into line.

Movement No. XIII. from Open Column.

Commanding Officer, repeated by Squadron Leader, *"Form Inverted Line to the Left on the First Squadron*."*

Leader of the First Squadron, *"First Squadron Left Wheel into Line."*

Commanding Officer, repeated by Squadron Leaders, *"Walk,* or *"Trot,* *March."*

On the word *"March,"* the First Squadron wheels left into line, receives the word *"Forward"* from its Leader, and, after advancing three horses' lengths, *"Halt, Dress."*

The Second and Third Squadrons pass successively along the rear of the First; each, as soon as it has got its proper interval from the right flank of that which preceded it, receives from its Leader the words *"Left wheel into Line, Forward;"* and, when on a line with the rear rank of the last-formed Squadron, *"Halt, Dress up."*

OBSERVATIONS. The object of this Movement is to show an immediate and successively increasing Front to the pivot flank, in less time than it could be done by moving the whole Column forward, and wheeling it into Line in its natural order. This Movement should, therefore, be considered one of necessity, not of convenience, and should be had recourse to as the readiest means of formation, under the circumstances of the moment. When the Column is considerable (as in Brigade), and time permits, it will be better to invert by Regiments instead of by Squadrons, each Regiment wheeling into line in succession.

---

* The Base is given by the Marker and Left Troop Leader of the First Squadron, when wheeled into Line.

Movement No. XIV. from Open Column.

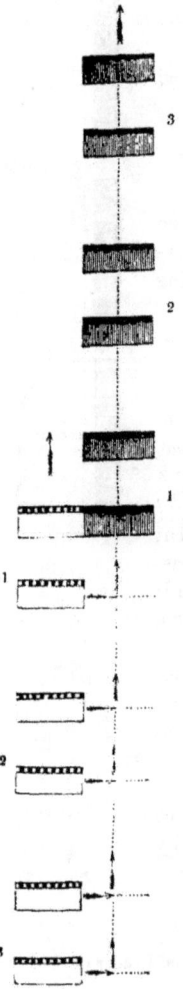

Commanding Officer, repeated by Squadron Leaders, { "*Rear of the Column to the Front.*" }

Leader of the Rear Troop, { "*Left Troop, Threes Right.*" }

Commanding Officer, repeated by Squadron Leaders, { "*Walk,* or "*Trot,*" } *March.*"

On the word "*March,*" the Rear Troop moves out to the right, and as soon as it is clear of the Column receives the words "*Halt, Front, Forward,*" from its Leader, and then advances.

The others follow in succession, each Leader giving the word "*Threes Right,*" followed by "*March,*" as soon as the advance of the preceding Troop enables him to pass close behind it, and then "*Halt, Front, Forward,*" when he covers in Column.

Each Troop must make its Flank March at an increased pace, in order to insure a correct preservation of distances.

OBSERVATION. The Troops may be wheeled "*Threes Left,*" and led out to the pivot flank, if circumstances render it necessary; but the word "*By the pivot flank*" must in such case be added to the caution.

Movement No. XV. from Open Column.

Commanding Officer, repeated by Squadron Leaders, } "*Form Close Column.*"

Leader of the Right Troop of the First Squadron, } "*Right Troop Advance.*"

Leaders of Left Troops of each Squadron, } "*Left Troop Left Incline.*"

Commanding Officer, repeated by Squadron Leaders, { "*Walk,*" or "*Trot,*" } *March.*"

On the word "*March,*" the Leading Troop advances three horses' lengths, and receives from its Leader the word "*Halt, Dress.*"

The other Right Troops move straight forward.

The Left Troops incline to their left, at double the pace, till their right flanks are uncovered; they then receive the word "*Forward*" from their Leaders, followed by "*Halt, Dress up,*" from the Leader of the Left Troop of the First Squadron, and "*Walk*" from the other Leaders of Left Troops as they come into Line with their Right Troops.

Each Squadron, as soon as formed, receives the word "*Eyes Left*" from its Leader, and, when moved up to its proper distance in Close Column, "*Halt Dress.*"

Movement No. XVI. from Double Column.

Commanding Officer, repeated by Squadron Leaders, } "*Form Line to the Front*.*"

Leader of the Second Squadron, "*Second Squadron Advance.*"

Leader of the First Squadron, "*Troops Half Right.*"

Leader of the Third Squadron, "*Troops Half Left.*

Commanding Officer, repeated by Squadron Leaders, { "*Walk,* or "*Trot,* } *March.*"

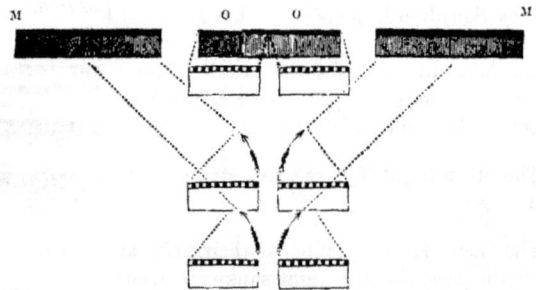

On the word "*March,*" the two centre Troops advance three horses' lengths, closing to the centre on the move (if of the same Squadron), and receive from the Squadron Leader the word "*Halt, Dress.*"

The Troops of the Right Column wheel half-right, those of the Left half-left; and, receiving from Squadron Leaders the word "*Forward,*" advance, in echellon, towards their places in the Line, and form as prescribed in Movement No. II.

In case an even number of Squadrons is to perform this Movement, the Base is given by the Leaders of the two Troops at the head of the Column.

---

* The Base is given by the Troop Leaders of the Second Squadron.

Movement No. XVII. from Double Column.

Commanding Officer, repeated by Squadron Leaders, } "*Form Line to the Right*.*"

Leader of the First Squadron and Leader of the Right Troop of the Second Squadron, } "*Right Wheel into Line.*"

Commanding Officer, repeated by Squadron Leaders, } { "*Walk,* or "*Trot,*" } *March.*"

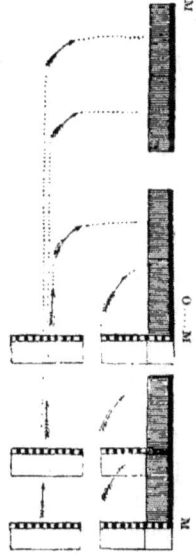

On the word "*March,*" the Troops of the Right Column wheel right into line, and are halted and dressed by Squadron Leaders.

The Troops of the Left Column pass along the rear of the formed Line, and form as prescribed in Movement No. X.

---

* The Base is given by the Marker and Right Troop Leader of the Second Squadron.

Section XIV. SKIRMISHING.

The usual object of employing Skirmishers is either to gain time, to watch the movements of the Enemy, to keep him in check, or to prevent him approaching so close to the main body as to annoy the line of march. Regularity in Skirmishing and correctness of distance cannot always be maintained, on account of the nature of the ground. It is nevertheless essential that some general rules should be laid down for Instruction, which, when become habitual, are easily conformed to, and applied according to circumstances.

1. Skirmishers are posted on the flanks of the Squadron, a few selected men being appointed for this duty.

2. When the Trumpet sounds for Skirmishers, they spread out at once in a Single Rank, Rear Rank on the left of their Front Rank men, at intervals of about twenty yards from each other, covering the front of the Regiment at a distance of from 150 to 200 yards, and outflanking it about 80 or 100 yards.

3. The Skirmishers are commanded by a Subaltern, assisted by two Non-commissioned Officers, the Subaltern remaining near the Centre and the Non-commissioned Officers near the Flanks.

4. Squadrons acting as Advance or Rear Guards detach a small party in support of their Skirmishers.

5. Skirmishers should be trained to act rather by mutual understanding of the objects for which they are employed than by any too confined system; and above all, they must be instructed to look to the nature of the ground. They should always keep their horses in motion, even when loading, to avoid becoming a mark to their opponents.

6. Although one Rank is most advisable for the Advance, yet on occasions of Retreat it is best for Skirmishers to form and act in two Ranks (supporting each other); as, for instance, in retiring across Ravines, Rivers, or other localities, where one Rank is thus enabled to protect the retreat of the other.

In retiring, the Front Rank leads to the Rear, and fronts at the distance of forty or fifty yards; the other Rank, after firing, does the same: thus the two lines retire through each other (bridle hand to bridle hand), alternately forming and supporting. The line nearest the Enemy must never fire till the other has loaded and fronted.

7. To retire, the word of command is *"About;"* to face the Enemy, *"Front;"* to take ground to a flank, *"Files Right,"* or *"Files Left."* These words of command (which ought to be very sparingly used) are always accompanied by a wave of the Sword, indicating the direction.

8. Skirmishers must be very exact and alert in noticing, and instantly obeying, the signals made for their guidance, whether proceeding from their own Commander or from the Trumpet.

9. In Flank Movements, the Skirmishers cover the front and flank of the Column nearest the Enemy by filing to the right or left, the alternate man giving a low word *"Ready"* to the man who precedes him, as soon as loaded.

10. When recalled, the Skirmishers must trot steadily back to their Squadrons, pass through the intervals, and form up without hurry.

11. Galloping should be avoided by Skirmishers. In retiring especially they should always avoid any appearance of haste or confusion.

12. It should be impressed upon the men when ordered to fire, to level low, and never to fire without deliberate aim. Random shots over the heads of a mob are unjustifiable, because likely to injure persons quite unconcerned in the riot.

Section XV.

ADVANCE GUARDS AND REAR GUARDS.

Advance Guards should never be dispensed with on the most ordinary Marches; and no Corps, Column, or detached Body whatever, is to neglect this military precaution for its safety.

1. The strength of Advance Guards should be in proportion to the body from which they are detached; for instance, one Troop may be generally considered as sufficient for three Squadrons.

2. The Advance Guard usually marches about two hundred or two hundred and fifty yards in front of the Column, but the distance must entirely depend on circumstances, and whether the country is open or inclosed; also, whether it is in the night, or in foggy and thick weather. The Advance Guard detaches a party of about one-third to its front; this party sends forward a smaller one, and from this last two men precede the whole. As a general rule, an Advance Guard should constantly be in communication with, or in sight of, the party from whence it is detached.

3. Rear Guards, in cases of retreat, are formed on the same principles, in respect to disposition and number, as Advance Guards on a march to the front; but their duties are confined to preventing the surprise of the rear. Detachments from the Rear Guard must never entirely lose sight of the party to which they belong.

Section XVI.

ARRANGEMENTS ON OCCASION OF RIOTS OR GENERAL DISTURBANCES.

It is by Troops or Detachments that Yeomanry are usually called upon in aid of the civil power. The suppression of riots, the protection of property, and the escorting of prisoners, are the duties they are most usually wanted to perform: they are therefore, when serious riots unhappily occur, peculiarly liable to act under difficulties which are severe trials of discipline. Narrow lanes, hollow roads, and intricate inclosures, are situations where the utmost steadiness and precaution must be observed to prevent confusion, and no little judgment is required under such circumstances. For these reasons, it is strongly recommended, that when detachments are employed on this sort of service, the formation should be in single rank, by which much difficulty to the young soldier is removed, and infinitely greater facility of movement and of acting in confined spaces is attained. The formation in single rank is not only advantageous for movements in narrow lanes and defiles, &c., but when drawn up, as will frequently be the case, in the vicinity of farm-yards, or manufactories, it enables every man, if necessary, to use his carbine or pistol, which, when formed two deep, the rear rank cannot do without risk. Besides which, they are themselves less exposed to stones or other missiles, than when in double rank, and their appearance is more formidable from their apparently greater numbers. Against an unorganized and tumultuous mob, a rear rank may be considered not only unnecessary, but it will even prove a disadvantage and positive inconvenience. So far from the habit of forming and exercising in single rank rendering Yeomanry less competent to move with the Cavalry of the Line when required, or less handy when formed on other occasions with two ranks, it may be as well to observe, that the regiments of regular Cavalry are particularly instructed to exercise frequently in single rank, as the best possible preparation for field movements on a greater scale.

On the first breaking out of riot, everything depends on the promptitude with which an armed force can be displayed upon the spot. Every hour lost is an accession of confidence and numbers to the rioters, while it adds to the confusion of the well-disposed, and augments the real danger by the promulgation of exaggerated reports. The means for insuring the rapid assembly of a Yeomanry Corps, is a point deserving the utmost attention. Much must depend on the nature of the country and distances at which the individuals reside, but it will always be very easy to establish a system of ready communication and circulation of orders from some central point in the district, by which the Corps may be warned and assembled in an extremely short time, and for the reasons above stated, nothing can be more necessary and important.

Whenever Yeomanry are out upon any serious occasion, a certain number of men should be on picquet duty at some central house during both night and day, with a sentry on the look-out, and their horses saddled and (except when feeding) bridled, and one half only should feed at the same time. Occasional patrols should likewise be made, and if any sudden emergency be expected, a part or all of the whole Corps should remain saddled, according to circumstances.

An Alarm-post must always be fixed before each Troop is dismissed into quarters, at which it is to assemble in case of need: with this spot each man must be acquainted, and with the shortest and most direct road to it from his own quarters: he must also know the signal upon which he is to turn-out and proceed to the Alarm-post. In order to render these arrangements habitual, Alarm-posts ought always to be fixed upon as places of parading, when Yeomanry assemble, even on common occasions. The Alarm-posts should be in the most open, central, and easily-approached part of the town in which the Troops are stationed*. Where the Corps is a large one, each Troop and Squadron should have its separate post for assembly.

Three stable duties should be ordered daily of one hour each,

---

* When a town is in a state of actual riot, it may often be advisable to bivouac outside, rather than risk the dispersion of the men in billets.

ON RIOTS AND DISTURBANCES.

every man to be present; morning stable soon after day-break, mid-day stables about noon, and evening about sunset.

Although the weather should not admit of any field exercise, still, unless it is so extremely bad as to render it impossible for the men to assemble without probable injury to themselves, their horses, and appointments, it is highly necessary that a mounted parade should take place daily for the purpose of inspection.

No detachment should go out without an Officer, unless in case of sickness or unforeseen emergency; Escorts of course excepted, which, it may be here observed, ought never to consist of less than six men and a Non-commissioned Officer.

When the detachment at any station amounts to a Troop, the Officer should represent to the Magistrate by whom he may be called out, the great advantage of not employing more than half the men at a time, except on very urgent occasions, in order that a Reserve may be left in quarters for a further emergency, or in event of demand for assistance in another direction. In case of detachments of half a Troop or less, it is advisable that the whole should be taken out, in order to guard against too small a division of force. It is of importance at all times to have a Troop or Detachment, when in quarters, as closely connected as possible.

In event of any immediate apprehensions of disturbance in or near a station, at least one third of the detachment should be held at all times in readiness as a picquet, at one of the principal billets.

A feed of corn in a small nose bag is to be always held in readiness for each horse, and carried when the detachment is called out, also by any man sent on orderly duty. The most convenient way of carrying it is to suspend it behind the thigh by a strap from the cantle of the saddle. These bags should be of stout canvass or duck, either double, or painted outside to prevent the sweat of the horse from getting to the corn while hanging to the saddle.

The bridles, swords, and fire-arms should always be taken up by the men to their rooms at night; and all articles of saddlery should be so placed in the stable as to be readily laid hold of, in case of a sudden turn-out in the night.

Officers should endeavour, when employed at any distance from their own districts, to make themselves acquainted with the adjacent roads and country; also with the most direct communication to their head-quarters, and to the detachments both of Regular Troops and Yeomanry in their vicinity.

The rate of march must at all times be left to the discretion of the Officer commanding the force employed. In ordinary cases it is never to exceed the rate of six miles per hour. On very urgent occasions, and for a short distance, a detachment may move at the rate of eight miles an hour; but upon no occasion whatever is the rate of march to be such as to exhaust the horses, or to render them unfit for increased exertion upon their arrival at the point where their services are likely to be required.

Section XVII.

PRECAUTIONS ON THE MARCH.

In moving towards places where there are disturbances, there should always be both an advanced and rear guard, each consisting of two or three intelligent and well-mounted men, keeping a good look-out; those in advance examining the turns in the roads, the copses and plantations that are on either side of it, and the farm-yards and other places of that nature where a number of men might lie concealed. Between each of these detached parties and the main body, there should again be one or two men to keep up the communication, and give the alarm if necessary. The advanced and rear guard should have their fire arms in their hands and loaded: without these precautions the best Cavalry in the world are in danger of surprise and disgrace from a very few opponents well posted in hedges and such places of concealment.

It should be a general rule to march with columns of as wide a front as the road will admit without crowding, and to take care that the rear does not press too much upon the front. It

PRECAUTIONS ON THE MARCH.

must be recollected, that when acting in streets, roads, &c., the front of a column alone can be engaged; and that instead of what is called a well-closed-up column being of much use, as far as relates to Cavalry, it often leads to confusion, for it must be evident, that in case of the front being driven back, the more dense and compact the column, the more difficult will it be to restore it to any degree of order, after confusion has once begun in the front. Whenever, therefore, a column is on the march with any expectation of resistance, it should march in several detachments, with an interval between the rear of one detachment and the head of the next, of not less than forty or fifty yards, by which means, in case the leading detachmennt should meet with any disaster, it has those in the rear to fall upon for support, and without any risk of their being thrown into disorder, or taken by surprise.

This naturally leads to the injunction universally applicable to Cavalry, that in all circumstances of danger there must be a portion of the corps held strictly in reserve. It is a rule never to be neglected with impunity, especially when formed in line, and called upon to advance against a body of rioters. Steadiness and order will, in such cases, produce much more effect and intimidation than any misplaced impetuosity; and it must be recollected, never to permit more than one half of the line to advance for the dispersion of the rioters, the other half to remain as a reserve, perfectly steady, and halted, or following the advanced party at a walk or very gentle trot, in order that those in front may fall back if any disorder should arise in their ranks, and form again in their rear or on their flank.

It cannot be too much urged upon the attention of every Yeoman, that, when once disorder has arisen in the ranks of mounted Troops, it is more difficult to rally and re-form one single Squadron than a whole Regiment of Infantry. And they should also be aware that when once dispersion has taken place, even though a consequence of success, they cease to be formidable to such a degree, that a man on foot, if well armed, may keep off the attack of a single horseman, provided he faces him resolutely, and is not influenced by the imposing appearance of his opponent. On the other hand, as long as Cavalry maintain their ranks with steadiness and order, and do not expose themselves to fall into confusion, by attempting too great rapidity of movement, they are irresistible by any description of force except a thoroughly disciplined Infantry, formed in square to receive them.

In conclusion, it must be observed as not the least important part of this subject, that since difficulties arise in some instances from ignorance of the power of the Military to act, excepting under the personal direction of a Magistrate, in the preservation of the public peace and suppression of riots, it is right that all armed bodies should be aware of the recorded opinion of the law-officers of the Crown, that "Although it is advisable to procure a justice of the peace to attend, and for the Military to act under his orders, when such attendance can be obtained;" yet that, "in the event of a breach of the peace by an assembled multitude, any of his majesty's subjects, without the presence of a peace-officer, may arm themselves, and of course may use ordinary means of force to suppress such riot and disturbances, and that what his majesty's subjects may do, they also ought to do, for the suppression of public tumult, when an exigency may require that such means be resorted to; and whatever any other class of his majesty's subjects may allowably do in this particular, the Military may unquestionably do also."

Section XVIII. ESCORTS.

Yeomanry are frequently required to furnish Escorts in times of disturbance, for the transport of prisoners; and there is no occasion where more steadiness and precaution is necessary. The manner of forming such Escorts must greatly depend on circumstances, but the following may be taken for ordinary guidance, first observing that on all such occasions Yeomanry should be formed in single rank.

Suppose the case of a Troop of about fifty men ordered to form an Escort for a waggon or other conveyance, containing prisoners, the Commanding Officer forms his men in line, and proceeds to direct the flank Serjeant to move off with the two men next him, and form an advance guard, the two men preceding this Non-commissioned Officer about one hundred yards, and the latter keeping about the same distance in front of the Escort. The next three follow as an advanced party, about fifty yards behind the Non-commissioned Officer; fifty yards behind the advanced party follow the rest of the right division by threes, thus: four threes (twelve men) in front of the waggon; the next three, one behind the other, on the right-hand side of it; the next three in like order, on the left of it. These six men are called the Flankers. The left division or half Troop follows behind the waggon by threes; the left-flank Serjeant being about fifty yards in rear, with two men as a rear guard about one hundred yards behind him.

It must be observed, that the distances both of the advance and rear guard depend on the nature of the country to be passed through, being of course greater in an open country, and less in a district that is wooded or obstructed, making it always a rule that they should never be quite out of sight of the main body.

It is very advisable that the men should all keep their proper places by threes; therefore, if the moving off the flank Serjeant and his men for the advance guard breaks into the next three, as must be the case if there happens to be an incomplete three on that flank, the odd men should be attached to the advanced party, by which means the main body of the Escort will be able to march in their regular order by threes, and the whole can form up readily and without risk of confusion. Any odd men on the left flank should, on the same principle, be attached to that part of the Escort which follows immediately behind the waggon.

The Commanding Officer should in general remain near the prisoners; but he should constantly communicate by one of his Officers or Non-commissioned Officers with the advance and rear guards, to know if all is right with them. Any attempt to crowd in upon the prisoners must be quickly repressed by the Flankers, who, if the Escort is in a country road and accompanied by a crowd, should, if possible, prevent any people from keeping alongside, even on the foot-paths. The Officers should not be confined to any particular post, but be so distributed as to keep a general superintendence of the Escort.

One man of the advance guard should instantly, on discovering any obstacle to the march, whether accidental or intentional, ride back to the Commanding Officer, telling his Serjeant as he passes, and inform him exactly how matters stand. When interruption is expected, a few men of the main body should have their fire-arms loaded, and at the "Carry," instead of their swords. One of the advance guard should march with his fire-arms carried, and the other with his sword drawn; the same with respect to the rear guard.

In case of opposition, the main body of the Escort should always endeavour to keep moving forward; and unless considerable preparation has been made, no ordinary assemblage will be able to prevent mounted Troops advancing, if they preserve good order and silence, and move at a steady trot.

An Officer charged by the civil power with the escort of prisoners should insist upon such a conveyance being provided as may enable the whole to move at a brisk pace, if circumstances should make it necessary.

The arrangement of a small detachment employed on Escort duty should be made as nearly as possible in conformity to what has been laid down for a Troop. The advance and rear guard, even although the strength of the detachment might not admit of more than one man for each of those duties, must never be dispensed with.

It is always advisable that one Commissioned Officer, at least, should accompany an Escort, however small. There are very few occasions where it would be proper or safe to employ fewer than ten or twelve men on this duty, especially if there are more than half that number of prisoners.

Constables should always be required to go in the conveyance with the prisoners, if possible.

Escorts of Honour.

Escorts or Guards of Honour are occasionally furnished by Yeomanry for royal personages*. They are usually formed facing the door-way at which the royal carriage is waiting, in single rank. On the royal personage's appearance at the door, the Commanding Officer gives the word "*Draw Swords,*" he and the other Officers saluting but quickly recovering their swords, and giving the word "*Threes Right,*" or "*Left,*" as the case may be, followed by "*Form the Escort, Trot, March,*" on which the whole, having been previously cautioned, move quickly to their respective posts, the two senior Officers placing themselves one by the side of each window of the carriage, the second Flankers either riding outside or following them.

As the carriage arrives at its destination, the Escort forms line, facing the gateway or door at which it stops, the Flankers dropping back, and taking their places by Threes, and the Officers regaining their stations in front of the line as it is forming, and immediately saluting.

It must be recollected, that if the carriage moves off towards the left flank of the Escort they march off left in front, but *vice*

---

* The order of march is the same as for the common Escort already described.

versâ, if the carriage moves off towards the right. If the door at which the carriage stops on arrival happens to be on the right, the Escort, if right in front, must form by the Advance guard wheeling up and halting short of the entrance, the remainder passing on behind them, and coming up successively to their places in the way laid down for the "Formation of the Squadron to the Reverse Flank" (page 78), whereas if the door at which the carriage is to stop is on the left hand side, the men of the advance guard move on past it, wheel up to their left, and halt, the remainder closing to them as they arrive, on the principle of "Left Form," as laid down in the "Formation of the Squadron" (page 77).

If the road leads up to an entrance door, directly facing it, the Advance guard inclines away to the right, (supposing they are marching right in front,) and halts, facing the house at such a distance to their right of the door as may bring the centre part of the Escort about opposite to it. The remainder as they arrive form upon the Advance guard as laid down in the "Formation to the Front" (page 72), taking care, however, not to impede the carriage as it passes out to the front of their line.

If Escorts, as is strongly recommended, are always formed in single rank, it must be borne in mind to take no account of what regards the rear rank, in referring to the Formations.

It has been thought advisable to enter into these minute details, because an Escort of Honour is an opportunity for Yeomanry to show their activity and good training; while, on the other hand, there is no occasion where mistakes and confusion are more likely to occur, and where the exposure of them is more conspicuous.

Order of March of an Escort.

The dark figures show the position of the Carriage, or Waggon, and its Horses, in the Line of March.

Advance Guard

Non-commissioned Officer

Advanced Party

Flanker   Flanker

Flanker   Flanker

Flanker   Flanker

Non-commissioned Officer

Rear Guard

N.B. In an Escort of Honour, the two Senior Officers take the places of the Centre Flankers, who then ride outside of them or behind them.

Section XIX.

OFFENCES AND FINES.

The application of the following scale to the customs and situations of particular Corps must of course be left to the judgment of Commanding Officers. The scale is merely suggested as a general rule, subject to modification; but whether all or only partly adopted, the system of fines, when once fixed, chould be unchangeable.

Regulated Fines according to Rank.

Commissioned Officers, 10s.

Non-commissioned Officers, 4s.

Privates, 2s.

Neglecting to attend unless prevented by illness, of which a medical certificate must be sent; the whole of the regulated fine according to rank.

For every quarter late of the first hour after Roll Call, each Rank to forfeit one fourth of the regulated fine, for non-attendance.

After the expiration of the first hour, no member should be allowed to fall in at all.

Any Serjeant not having a written copy of the Roll Call with him on Parade, 1s.

When the Troop assembles two or more successive days, the fine to be increased one half for each successive day of absence.

The following offences to be fined in the proportion of one-fourth of the regulated fine, according to rank:

Leaving the Ranks without permission during "Attention."

Talking in the Ranks.

OFFENCES AND FINES.

Appearing on parade with clothes, arms, or accoutrements incomplete, or improperly put on.

Appearing with the horse appointments dirty, or with cloak or accoutrements improperly put on.

Disobedience of orders, or any disrespect shown to any Officer, will be instantly reported to the Officer commanding the Corps; and it is earnestly to be impressed upon all ranks, that so much of discipline depends upon the obedience of Non-commissioned Officers, that not only must all Commissioned Officers see that it is always duly paid them, but these Officers themselves must be instantly reduced, if they do not report any contempt or neglect of their authority.

Drunkenness on parade is a fault so degrading and disgraceful to the whole Corps, that, although a fine for the *first* offence may be accepted, a repetition of the offence should invariably be punished by expulsion.

Clothing and Accoutrements.

Whoever suffers any part of his uniform, arms, or accoutrements to be injured or defaced, unless by unavoidable accident when on duty, must furnish himself with new ones, or bear the expense of such repair as will make them appear in every respect the same as those of the rest of the Corps.

If the arms or accoutrements require repair or alteration, the same is to be reported to the Commanding Officer of the Troop, and any person who shall have any alteration made, without such communication, shall pay his regulated fine according to rank.

Any Non-commissioned Officer or Private wearing any article of his military equipment, except when on duty, shall for each offence pay his regulated fine according to rank.

No member shall exchange his clothes, arms, or accoutrements with another, without the consent of his Commanding Officer, under penalty of a double fine according to rank.

Extra Penalties for Non-attendance on Occasions of aiding the Civil Power.

Commissioned Officers, 5*l.*

Non-commissioned Officers, 2*l.*

Privates, 1*l.*

In the event of a Troop being called out in aid of the civil power, it will be the duty of every member to render all assistance to the District Serjeants and Corporals in making the same known to the persons belonging to his Troop, and to repair with as little delay as possible to Head Quarters, or the Troop Alarm-Post; should a member be absent from home at the time of the order, he will repair to join his Troop without loss of time on his return, fully accoutred, and provided for duty.

All fines to be paid to the Quarter-Master of the Troop on the following parade day.

The names of defaulters, on all days of assembly, to be read to the Troop, before dismissal.

The fines will be appropriated for the use and benefit of the Troop.

If any person shall consider himself aggrieved by the imposition of any fine, he shall privately, or by writing, make the same known to his Captain, who will refer the disputed point to the Commandant.

Any member shall, at any time, be at liberty to quit the Corps, on giving *fourteen days'* notice of his intention, in writing, to the Captain of his Troop.

——————— on delivering up to such Captain his clothes.

——————— on paying the amount of damage they may have sustained beyond the reasonable wear and tear.

——————— on returning his arms and accoutrements.

——————— and on paying up such fines as may be owing by him at the time of receiving his discharge.

Extract from an Act of 43rd Geo. III., cap. 121, *intituled "An Act, &c., &c., for the further regulating of Yeomanry and Volunteer Corps,"* Sect. 14.

" And be it further enacted, that where any person enrolled in any such corps shall have neglected or refused, on demand made for that purpose, to pay any fines or penalties incurred under any of the rules and regulations thereof, then and in such case it shall be lawful for any justice of the peace, on application made for that purpose, and proof thereof by any Commanding Officer, &c., &c., to cause the same, together with double the amount thereof, as a penalty or forfeiture, to be levied by distress and sale of the defaulter's goods and chattels, by warrant under his hand and seal, &c., &c. And the sums so levied shall go to the general stock of such Corps, to be applied to such purposes relating to such Corps as the Commanding Officer thereof may think fit."

Section XX.

ABSTRACT OF THE GOVERNMENT REGULATIONS.

All matters not provided for in these Regulations must be referred to the Secretary of State for the Home Department, through the Lieutenant of the County.

Composition of Yeomanry.

No Troop must consist of less than 40, or more than 100 Privates (Farriers included).

Troops under 70 men have 1 Captain, 1 Lieutenant, 1 Cornet, 1 Quarter-Master, 1 Trumpeter: and Troops exceeding 70 have an additional Lieutenant.

A Serjeant and a Corporal are allowed to every 20 Privates; a Drill Serjeant is included in the number.

A Corps of 120 Privates is allowed a Serjeant-Major.

A Regiment of 300 Privates is allowed an Adjutant instead of a Serjeant Major.

A Corps or Regiment of 200 Privates is allowed 1 Lieutenant-Colonel and 1 Major.

A Regiment of 320 Privates is allowed a Lieutenant-Colonel Commandant, a Lieutenant-Colonel, and a Major.

Qualifications and Pay of Adjutant and Serjeant-Major.

ADJUTANT.—Four years' service as a Commissioned Officer or Serjeant-Major in the Regulars, Embodied Militia, Fencibles, or Honourable Company's Service. His pay is 6s. a day, besides 2s. for forage, and commences from his first day's duty.

SERJEANT-MAJOR.—Three years' service as a Non-commissioned Officer in the Regulars, Embodied Militia, or Fencibles. His pay is 3s. 2d. a day, besides 2s. for forage, and commences from his first day's duty. The application for permanent pay of a Serjeant-Major must be made to the War-Office, along with a statement of his service, and a certificate of his attestation, in the Yeomanry.

Returns and Applications.

The following Return, signed by the Commanding Officer for the Troop, Corps, or Regiment, is to be sent three times a year to the Home Secretary, viz., 1st April, 1st August, 1st December.

ABSTRACT OF GOVERNMENT REGULATIONS. 215

RETURN of the Number of Persons now Enrolled and Serving in the { Troop / Squadron / Corps / Regiment } of Yeomanry,

Commanded by ————, 1st of ————, 183 .

	Lieut.-Colonel.	Major.	Captain.	Lieutenant.	Cornet.	Adjutant.	Surgeon.	Assist.-Surgeon.	Vet.-Surgeon.	Quar.-Master.	Serjeant-Major.	Serjeants.	Corporals.	Trumpeters.	Farriers.	Privates.	Total
Number Serving.........																	
Wanting to complete ...																	
Establishment.........																	

I hereby certify this to be a correct Return.

J———— D————, *Commandant.*

On the following points application must always be made through the Lieutenant of the County, who, if he approves of the application, forwards it to the Home Secretary; No. 7 excepted, which he forwards to the Ordnance.

1. Alteration in the title or establishment of the Corps.

2. Permanent pay for an Adjutant.

3. Assembly for *Exercise*. This must always be accompanied by a statement of the intended date and place of assembly, the number of men, and the days of exercise, (not exceeding fourteen, nor less than five.) On the Home Secretary notifying his assent, the Lieutenant of the County signs this statement, and sends it to the War Office, from whence forms of estimate and account are then sent to the Commandant.

4. Assembly for *Permanent Duty*. This application goes through the same form, and is accompanied by the same kind of return as the last.

5. Officers' commissions.

6. Application for permanent pay for an Adjutant, (accompanied by statement of service.)

7. Supply or exchange of arms or accoutrements, (accompanied by a return of the effective strength of the Corps.)

On receiving through the Lieutenant of the County the authority for *Assembly for Exercise*, the Commandant transmits through the same channel a return, showing the intended date and place of assembly, the number of men, and the number of days.

An Officer on receiving his commission must without delay transmit to the *Gazette* writer, through the Clerk of the Peace for the County, the particulars of rank and date, signed by the Lieutenant for the County. The fee upon a commission is 5*s*.

Ordnance Supplies.

Carbines (12 per Troop)*.

Pistols, swords, belts, and sword-knots.

Trumpets or bugles, with strings.

Practice ammunition is supplied in the proportion of six

---

* It is expected that this limitation will be removed shortly, and every man allowed a carbine.

rounds of ball, sixteen of blank cartridge, and three flints to each man, due March 25; and four rounds of ball, eight of blank cartridge, and two flints, due September 29, every year. It is supplied half yearly by the Ordnance Office, on a requisition, in the annexed form, being made before the 1st of August for the next Spring allowance, and before the 1st of December for the next Autumn allowance. If the requisition is delayed beyond those periods, the allowance is forfeited.

RETURN of Ammunition Required for the {Spring / Autumn} Supply for the Exercise and Practice of the —— {Regiment / Corps / Squadron / Troop} of Yeomanry Cavalry.

The Effectives at the date of this Return are Rank and File.		Ball Cartridges.		Blank Cartridges.		Flints.	
		Carbine.	Pistol.	Carbine.	Pistol.	Carbine.	Pistol.
Arms in possession of the Corps, and their Calibre. Carbines. | Pistols.	Spring / Autumn } Allowance of Ammunition for Exercise and Practice, received on the day of						
	Expended in Exercise and Practice........						
Carbine Bore.	Remaining unexpended and Serviceable	—	—	—	—	—	—
	Wanted to complete the Proportion allowed by the Regulations						
	Total Allowance						

Head Quarters, Day of { I do hereby certify, that the above Return is correct in every respect.

(Signed)   J———— D————, Commanding.

No ammunition must be transferred from one Corps to another.

When out on *actual service* the necessary ammunition must be obtained by application to the General commanding in the District.

Commandants may buy clothing and appointments from the public stores, by application to the Ordnance.

A return of arms and stores in possession of the Regiment, Corps, Squadron, or Troop, must be sent on the 1st of November, yearly, to the Ordnance Office.

All correspondence regarding pay and allowances takes place with the Secretary at War, under this address:

Yeomanry Cavalry.	*The Right Honourable* THE SECRETARY AT WAR, *War Office,* London.

In replying to any War-Office letters the number as well as date must be quoted.

Forms are every year sent from the War Office to the Commandants, to be filled up with the number of days of exercise and duty performed. They must be filled up and returned within one month after receipt.

Contingent Allowance Annually.

For each effective Non-commissioned Officer, Trumpeter, Farrier, and Private, on the establishment, (including Drill Serjeant's pay,) but not that of the Serjeant Major, 1*l.* 10*s.*

Clothing and Appointments' Allowance.

Same as above, only *including* the Serjeant-Major.

Both these allowances, as well as the Adjutant and Serjeant-Major's pay, are issued half yearly in advance, on the Commandant's filling up and returning the form sent him for the purpose, from the War Office.

Three years of the contingent and clothing allowances will be advanced to new Regiments, Corps, Squadrons, or Troops, and also to augmentations of old ones, on applying for filling up and returning a War-Office form. But in both cases the men must be certified as enrolled and equipped within two months after the "Acceptance of Service."

Commandants of Regiments, Corps, or Squadrons, will receive all contingent and clothing balances from the Captains of Troops, and will draw for all arrears. This only applies to those Regiments or Corps formed of incorporated Troops.

Assembly.

The distinction between assembly for exercise, and assembly for permanent duty, must be carefully observed. In neither case must the actual assembly take place till the Lieutenant of the county has sent the Commandant, in writing, the consent of the Home Secretary.

For Exercise.

Yeomanry are not allowed to assemble for exercise for less than five consecutive days, nor must the whole of the days within the year exceed fourteen. Therefore, if they assemble more than twice in the year, special leave must be obtained, at one of the periods, to meet for four days in lieu of five.

The pay when assembled for exercise is 2*s.* for each man, and 1*s.* 4*d.* for each horse daily.

In ten days after the assembly for exercise is over, the Commandant sends to the Secretary-at-War an account of sums paid, and sums received, from whom he then receives either a form of bill to draw for whatever has fallen short, or an order to pay whatever may have remained over in his hands to the Bank of England.

For Permanent Duty,

May be substituted for assembly for exercise. It must not exceed six consecutive days, besides the days of marching to and from the assembly. Immediately on receiving, through the Lieutenant of the County, the leave to assemble, estimates for the pay and allowances are to be sent to the War Office, on the forms supplied from thence; and in return a bill at ten days' sight is sent to the Commanding Officer. Within ten days after the duty is over, the account must be sent to the War Office; on which the Secretary-at-War, if he approves the account, either remits the balance due, if the bill did not suffice, or directs the balance over to be paid to Government, if the bill more than covered the expenditure. Yeomanry thus assembled are under the General of the District's orders, if there is one, or if in a garrison, under those of the Commandant, and are to conform to the Regulations for the Regulars. The Articles of War are to be read to the Yeomanry on these occasions.

Yeomanry when assembled on permanent duty, or in aid of the civil power, are billeted the same as regular Cavalry.

Aid of Civil Power.

The order of the Lieutenancy or Magistracy calling out Yeomanry, in aid of the Civil Power, should state the reasons for so doing, and number of Troops required on these occasions*. The same daily rate of pay is allowed as when on "Permanent Duty."

A copy of the order is to be instantly sent by the Commandant to the Secretary-at-War, with an application for forms of esti-

---

* Of course when the case is immediate, a mere informality of the order in these respects would be no excuse for delay.

mate and account. After the duty is performed, and the account made up, it is to be transmitted to the Secretary-at-War with this certificate:

We, the undersigned Magistrates for the   of
   do hereby certify that   Troops of the
Yeomanry Cavalry were assembled in aid of the civil power
on the   of   , and that the said Troops
were actually and necessarily required by the civil authorities to remain on duty from that date until the   of
                             Magistrates for the
                             of
                             residing at

Points to be observed in drawing and negotiating Bills upon the Paymaster-General.

[Extracted from War-Office Orders of Jan. 1, 1831.]

When an estimate or account is approved, a form of bill for the sum, which the Paymaster-General may be authorized to issue, will be transmitted from the War Office to the proper Officer, for negotiation.

No Officer is allowed to draw any bill upon the Paymaster-General, but upon the very form which he shall have received from the War Office, with the exact sum to be drawn by him already inserted therein.

No bill must under any circumstances be signed by any other person than the Officer who shall have been expressly authorized by the War Office to draw the bill.

The *printed* letter of advice, annexed to the authority, must be carefully filled up, signed *by the drawer of the bill*, and transmitted to the War Office, by the post of the day on which it was negotiated.

The letters of advice must exactly agree with the bill, in the particulars of its *date*, the *amount*, and the *names of the parties to whom it is made payable.*

In filling up the bill, the *name* of the *party* or *firm* to whom it is payable must be *accurately spelt;* the amount in the body of the bill must be distinctly *stated in words at length*, and must exactly agree with the amount stated in figures in the margin: these points deserve particular attention, as inaccuracies, *especially where the name or firm in the body of the bill differs from the endorsement*, will prevent the payment by the Bank of England, although the bill be duly accepted by the Paymaster-General.

When bills are returned unpaid by the Bank of England, on account of irregularity, after having received the Paymaster-General's acceptance, they must on no account be destroyed, but the irregularity must be corrected, and the bill again presented for payment, as the Paymaster-General, having once given his acceptance on behalf of the public, cannot give it a second time for the same sum.

In the event of a bill being accidentally defaced prior to acceptance, no other can be substituted by the Accountant, but application must be made to the War Office for a new form, and the bill so defaced must be returned to that department.

As by a proper attention to the Regulations and the foregoing Memoranda, *no Officer need ever be exposed to the inconvenience of having his bills returned*, any expense which may arise in cases where irregularity occurs must be borne by the drawers.

Section XXI.

Schedule of the Pay and Allowances of the Yeomanry Cavalry while doing Permanent Duty, or Duty in Aid of the Civil Power.

PAY.		Rates of Consolidated Pay and Allowances per Diem.	CONTINGENT ALLOWANCES.
		£ s. d.	
An Allowance of 2s. 8d. a Day per Troop is also made to the Colonel, or to the Officer having a Commission as Commandant.	Colonel	1 12 10	To defray the expense of Postage and Stationery, and other Charges incidental to making up the Accounts, viz.
	Lieutenant-Colonel	1 3 0	£ s. d.
	Major	0 19 0	For a Corps consisting of { 1 Troop, per Diem 0 1 0
	Captain (including his Allowance of 2s. 2d. per Diem)	0 16 9	2 Troops...... 0 1 1
			3 or 4 Troops... 0 1 7
During a Vacancy in the command of a Troop, 2s. 2d. a Day will be allowed for the repair of Arms and other expenses, to which the Allowance to the Captain is applicable	Lieutenant	0 9 0	For a Regiment consisting of 5, 6, or 7 Troops 0 1 10
	Cornet	0 8 0	For ditto consisting of 8 Troops or upwards 0 2 1
			Divine Service.—No allowance is granted unless a separate Service is absolutely requisite. In such cases the Clergyman is to apply to the War Office for remuneration.
These Rates only to be allowed in the whole, whether the Officers hold other Commission or not	Adjutant (including constant Pay and Allowances)	0 10 0	*Ferries.*—The actual expense incurred in passing Ferries, supported by the proper Vouchers, will be allowed.
	Surgeon	0 11 4	*Medicines furnished to the Sick.*—The actual expense thereof will be allowed, provided the Charge made be previously approved by the Director-General of the Army Medical Department, St. James's Place, London.
	Assistant-Surgeon	0 8 6	
	Quarter-Master	0 5 6	
In lieu of every other Charge whatsoever	Serjeant-Major (including constant Pay and Allowances)	0 7 0	*Compensation for Horses.*—The value of the Horse, not exceeding Thirty pounds, will be granted to the owner thereof, upon the application of the Commandant of the Corps, provided the Secretary-at-War shall be satisfied that the loss was entirely and inevitably occasioned by the act of duty in the performance of which the Horse was injured.
	Serjeant	0 7 0	
	Corporal	0 7 0	
	Trumpeter	0 7 0	
	Private	0 7 0	
Including the allowance for Farriery	Allowance in lieu of Forage for each effective Officer's horse, not exceeding the proportions for each rank*	0 1 6	The application is to be accompanied by a detailed statement of the circumstances of the case, certified by the Commandant, and by a Certificate of the value of the Horse.

* Proportion of Horses for each Rank:
Field Officer . . . not exceeding 4
Captain 3
Subaltern 2

Adjutant	not exceeding 3
Surgeon	2
Assistant-Surgeon	1
Quarter-Master	1

Section XXII.

DESTRUCTION OR LOSS OF ARMS.

"The cause of all deficiencies should be particularly noted when they happen; and when arms become unserviceable, they are not, on that account, to be destroyed, but reserved to be returned to the Ordnance, when a convenient opportunity shall arise." Subjoined is a statement of some of the amounts fixed by the Ordnance, to be charged to individuals, in case of the *wilful destruction* or *loss* by *neglect*, of any of the accoutrements furnished by the Government; the same being recoverable by a summary process at law.

	s.	d.
For each carbine	40	0
For each sword	13	0
For each sword scabbard	5	0
For each waist-belt	2	6
For each sword-knot	1	0
For each pistol	26	4
For each carbine ball cartridge	0	$0\frac{3}{4}$
For each pistol ditto	0	$0\frac{1}{2}$
For each flint	0	$0\frac{1}{4}$

SECTION XXIII.—County of _____

RETURN of the _____ Yeomanry Cavalry, under the Command of _____

Accepted Strength of the Corps.	Established per Troop.								Effective Strength of the Corps.								Number of Arms, Accoutrements, &c., supplied by Government, with the Date when received, and from whence.							Number of Arms, Accoutrements, &c. purchased by the Corps, and for which Government has granted the regulated Allowance.							Number of Arms, Accoutrements, &c. purchased by the Corps, for which no Allowance will be claimed.							REMARKS. State of the Arms, &c.
	Number of Troops	Quarter-Master	Serjeant-Major	Serjeants	Corporals	Trumpeters	Privates	Total	Number of Troops	Quarter-Master	Serjeant-Major	Serjeants	Corporals	Trumpeters	Privates	Total	DATE and PLACE whence received	Carbines	Pistols	Swords	Belts and Knots	Trumpets & Strings	Bugles	Carbines	Pistols	Swords	Belts and Knots	Trumpets & Strings	Bugles	Carbines	Pistols	Swords	Belts and Knots	Trumpets & Strings	Bugles	
																	Total · ·																			

I do hereby certify, that the above is a correct Return of the Effective Strength of the Corps under my Command, and of the Number and State of Arms, Accoutrements, &c., in its Possession.

Dated _____

Head Quarters } _____

London:
Parker, Furnivall, and Parker,
PUBLISHERS,
Military Library, Whitehall.

YEOMANRY REGULATIONS.

ERRATA, CORRECTIONS, & SUBSTITUTIONS,

AS REQUIRED BY THE

REVISED EDITION OF THE CAVALRY REGULATIONS

OF THE 20TH MAY, 1851.

NOTE.—These Errata are so printed that they can either be inserted as an extra sheet at the end of the Yeomanry Regulations; or, the smaller alterations being made by hand wherever they occur throughout the book, the substituted passages and pages can be cut out and pasted over the parts they are intended to supersede.

LONDON:
PARKER, FURNIVALL, AND PARKER,
MILITARY LIBRARY, WHITEHALL.

ERRATA

TO THE

YEOMANRY REGULATIONS.

September 1851.

P. 5, line 2 from foot—omit "*Half-cock Arms.*"
P. 6, line 2 from foot—for "left" read, right,
P. 22, line 9 from top—omit "*Leading Threes,*"
    line 8 from foot—omit "*Leading Threes,*"
P. 82, line 3 from top—insert "*Left Troop,*"
    line 7 from top—insert "*Right Troop,*"
    Art. 1, read the Command thus—
    "*Advance in Column of Troops from the Right.*"
P. 83, Substitution for Art. 3.

3 If the Squadron is at once to march off to its front, in Column of Divisions, the Caution is given,

"*Advance by Divisions from the right.*"

The Right Troop Leader gives the word, "*First Division. Advance; Second Division, Right Wheel.*"

The Left Troop Leader gives the word, "*Third and Fourth Divisions, Right Wheel.*"

On the word, *March*, the First Division moves straight forward; the Second Division wheels and receives the words, "*Left Wheel*" and "*Forward*" from its Guide; the Third and Fourth Divisions receive the word, "*Forward,*" from the Troop Leader, and, when arrived at the angle, "*Left Wheel,*" and "*Forward,*" from the Troop Leader, and Division Guide.

P. 83, Art. 4, ... —after "*Advance by Threes from the Right*" insert "*Threes Right.*"

P. 85, Art. 3, ... —after "*Advance by Threes from the Right*" insert "*Threes Right*"

ERRATA AND CORRECTIONS.

P. 85, line 6 from foot—after "Leaders" insert on the word *March* and omit it after "*Right*"

P. 86, line 1 .... —after "Leaders" insert on the word *March*, and omit it after "him"

P. 89, Art. 8 .... —instead of "*Rear Division Left incline, Trot*," read on which the Right Troop Leader gives the word "*Second Division Left incline, Trot*," and the Left Troop Leader, "*Third and Fourth Divisions Left incline, Trot*"

P. 91, Art. 8, last line —omit *Ranks* in the Command.

Art. 9, ... —for "proper point" read, centre

Substitute for Art. 9. 9 HALT OF THE SQUADRON. At the word "*Halt, Dress*," both Officers and Men dress to the Centre, till they receive the word, "*Eyes Front.*"

When one movement is immediately to succeed another, a critical dressing should not be required.

P. 95, line 4 .... —for "Rights of Threes," read "Lefts of Threes,"

line 5 .... —for "left," read "right,"

P. 97, line 8 .... —for "Rights of Threes," read "Lefts of Threes,"

line 9 .... —for "left," read "right,"

P. 108, Addition to Art. 4.

.... When a Close Column takes ground to its Reverse flank, the Leaders of Troops on the Reverse hand, lead in front of their Pivots, moving out, when the Threes wheel, and resuming their posts when they front.

P. 109, Substitute for last sentence of Art. 10. The Troop Leader at the head of the Column rides in front of the Pivot Guide, and is answerable for the direction. The Squadron Leaders superintend the whole.

P. 113, Substitution for Art. 1.

1 The Markers to be employed for Regimental Movements are, The Adjutant, The Regimental Serjeant-Major, and one Non-Commissioned Officer for each Squadron, called the Squadron Marker.

ERRATA AND CORRECTIONS. 4

In Changes of Front, and in Formations of Line, the Troop Leader of the Base Troop is employed with the Squadron Marker to give the Base, and is placed by the Squadron Leader.

P. 113, Art. 2 ...... —for "In all dressing in Line" read when a line is being formed

P. 113, add to Art. 2. In all Dressing in Column, the Leaders will be at one horse's length from the pivot Guide, and facing the flank of the Column. When the Dressing is completed the Leaders give the word "*Eyes Front*," and then take post.

P. 113, Substitute for Art. 3. 3 When an accurate Dressing is required after an Advance in Line, the Caution is given, "*By the Squadron of Direction, Dress*," repeated by Squadron Leaders, on which the Officers of that Squadron move forward a horse's length: but do not turn their horses about. The Troop Leaders give the Base, and, with the Squadron Leader, are dressed by the Major, or Officer appointed.

On the word "*March*" the Men of the Squadron of Direction move up to their proper distance from their Officers; and the other Squadrons (Officers, and Men) take up the dressing at a walk, each Squadron receiving from its Leader the word, "*Eyes Front*," as soon as steady.

P. 115, Substitute for Art. 9. 9 When a Regiment forms Close Column, the Adjutant places the Base for the covering of the Pivots; he also places the Base when the Close Column changes its front, countermarches its Squadrons, reverses its front, or forms line to its flank.

P. 115, Substitute for Art. 10. 10 In Deployment the Base consists of the Adjutant and Regimental Marker, who are placed by the Major (immediately upon the Caution) in front of the Base Squadron, at one horse's length from the head of the Column; the Adjutant at the reverse flank, and the Regimental Marker at the Pivot.

P. 116, Art. 19.

When the Caution is given for a Brigade to deploy on one of the Squadrons of a central or rear Regiment, Commanding Officers are answerable for immediately sending up to the head of the Column, the Adjutant and Regimental Marker who form the Base

ERRATA AND CORRECTIONS.

(and are posted by a Staff Officer); also, the Marker of the Squadron next in front, and the Marker of the Squadron next in rear of the Base Squadron.

The Bases in the Plates of Close Column at pp. 211, 212, & 213, must be corrected by insertion of $+$ ... A, instead of M ... $+$.

P. 118, read the two first lines of the last Article thus—

The moment he sees B come into line with the Steeple, A stops his horse, giving the word "*Halt*" to B, and raising his sword.

P. 119, last line of Art. 1—for " whole Line of Officers," read Squadron Leaders, to whom their own Troop Leaders look for the dressing.

P. 120, Art. 10, ... —after "*Halt*," insert "*Dress*."

P. 126, Art. 12, last line but one—for "pivot," read "right."

P. 127, line 5 .... —after "*Forward*," insert "*Eyes Right*."

P. 128, line 2, in the Command,—omit "*Open*."

P. 139, Substitute for 10 first lines of the Description,

The Caution is given, "*Alignment on the —— Squadron*," repeated by Squadron Leaders, on which the Troop Leaders of that Squadron, raise their swords. The Right Troop Leader (if that flank is to be advanced) moves forward, and is halted and placed by the Major, or Officer appointed, according to the intended degree of change. The other Troop Leader squares his horse accordingly, and the Squadron Leader moves up into the line marked by them. On the word "*March*," the......

P. 140, line 3 from top—read the Squadron Leaders' word of command thus, "*Threes Right*"

P. 140, line 3 from foot—after, "Squadron Leaders" insert, giving the words "*Half Left*" and "*Forward*"

P. 142, line 3 from top—in the Squadron Leaders' command, omit followed by "*Leading Threes, Half Left*"

P. 142, line 3 of the description—after, "Squadron Leaders" insert, giving the words, "*Half Left*," and "*Forward*" and ......

P. 142, line 4 from foot—after "*Right Wheel*" insert, "*Forward*"

ERRATA AND CORRECTIONS.

P. 143, in the Command—omit "*Open*"

P. 144, in the Command—omit "*Open*"

P. 148, read the Command—"*Form Double Column in Rear of the Centre.*"

P. 149, Substitute for the latter part of the description,

......The First Squadron having wheeled "Threes Left," and received the word "*Half Left*," "*Forward*," and the Third Squadron, "Threes Right," and received the word "*Half Right*," "*Forward*," each Troop Leader goes to the pivot flank of his leading Threes, and conducts his Troop into Column; those of the Right Wing, themselves, halting where their right flanks will cover, allow their Troops to pass them, and then giving *Halt, Front, Dress,* take their posts in front of the Second Files from the right. Those of the Left Wing continue leading on, to where the heads of their Troops will stand when wheeled up, and then giving "*Halt, Front, Dress,*" also take their posts in front of the Second Files from the right.

P. 150, read the Command thus—

"*Column of Troops in Rear of the Right.*"

P. 150, line 5 .... —omit followed by "*Leading Threes Half Right.*"

P. 151, line 4 .... —after Threes Right, insert, "and received the words "*Half Right, Forward,*"

line 6 .... —omit, "when within a few yards of the pivot line, he rides forward,"

line 13 .... — after Infantry, insert, "or for purposes of Parade,"

P. 152, in the description—after "Threes Left," insert, "and received the words "*Half Right, Forward.*"

P. 153, line 1 .... —after Threes Right, insert, "and received the words "*Half Right, Forward,*"

line 5 .... —after "*Halt, Front,*" insert "*Dress,*"

P. 157, line 6 from foot—after "*Oblique Line to the Left,*" insert, "repeated by Squadron Leaders,"

P. 160, ... —after the Commanding Officer's Caution, insert, "Squadron Leaders, "*Threes Right*"

ERRATA AND CORRECTIONS.

P. 160, line 12 from foot—for "the Leaders dressing them from the right and then resuming their posts," read, and continues to advance by the Squadron of Direction, unless ordered to halt.

P. 161, line 4 .... —omit "*Leading Threes, Right Wheel.*"

.... —read the first line of the Description thus, on the word "*March*" each Squadron receiving the words "*Right Wheel Forward*"

in 4th and 5th line of the Description—for "First" read Second

line 6 from foot—omit "*Leading Threes,*"

P. 163, line 5 from foot—omit "or *Half;*" and after *Right*, insert, "repeated by Squadron Leaders,"

P. 165, line 1,......... —after Commanding Officer, insert, "repeated by Squadron Leaders,"

P. 166, line 1, ... —after Commanding Officer, insert, "repeated by Squadron Leaders,"

[Observe, that in all the Deployments, the Base is given by the Adjutant and Regimental Marker, placed by the Major.]

P. 167, lines 10 & 11 from top—omit (or *Half*) and after "*Left*" insert, "repeated by Squadron Leaders,"

P. 168, first line......... —after "Commanding Officer," insert, repeated by Squadron Leaders,

line 13 .... —after left, insert "as soon as it gets room,"

last line ...... —for paces, read, "yards,"

P. 169, read the top line thus—Commanding Officer, repeated by Squadron Leaders, "*Change Front to the Right.*"

P. 170, first line ...... —insert "Commanding Officer" repeated by Squadron Leaders.

last paragraph—for "Right Troops" read, Reverse Troops and for "inward flanks" read, pivot flanks

P. 171, first line ...... —after "Commanding Officer" insert, repeated by Squadron Leaders.

ERRATA AND CORRECTIONS.

P. 176, line 6 from top—for "Squadron Leaders" read, Leaders of Second and Third Squadrons

P. 177, line 4 from top—for "Squadron Leaders" read, Leaders of First and Second Squadrons

P. 178, line 6 .... —for "Squadron Leaders" read, Leaders of First and Third Squadrons

P. 179, line 4 .... after "Leaders of," insert, Second and Third,

P. 180, read the first line thus—The other Troops having received the words "*Half Left Forward*" are conducted by......

Substitute for the five last lines of the description,

......" As each Troop successively arrives at its Marker, the Leader gives the words, *Left Wheel, Forward*, and then taking his post in front of the centre, *Halt, Front, Dress*, when the head of his Troop arrives at its place."

P. 181, line 4 .... —after "Leaders of" insert First and Second

P. 182, line 4 .... —for "Leaders of Squadrons," read, Leader of First Squadron,

line 6 .... —for "Leaders of Squadrons behind the Base," read, Leader of Third Squadron

www.ingramcontent.com/pod-product-compliance
Lightning Source LLC
Chambersburg PA
CBHW060504090426
42735CB00011B/2105